PICTORIAL HISTORY
City of Sydney

Alan Sharpe

KINGSCLEAR BOOKS

Books by Alan Sharpe
Nostalgia Australia
Colonial New South Wales
Years of Change
Shark Down Under
Bushranger Country
50 Crimes That Shocked Australia
Pictorial History: Manly to Palm Beach
Pictorial History: Newtown
Pictorial History: Blacktown

© Kingsclear Books ABN 99 001 904 034
kingsclear@wr.com.au
www.kingsclearbooks.com.au
P.O. Box 335 Alexandria 1435
Phone (02) 9557 4367 Facsimile (02) 9557 2337

© Copyright 2000 Kingsclear Books

ISBN 0 908272 63 4

This book is copyright.
No part can be reproduced without written permission from the publisher.

First printed 2000, reprinted 2005
Printed in China by Everbest Printing Co Ltd

Contents

Sydney Cove	1
Circular Quay	4
The Rocks	16
The Harbour Bridge	23
The Opera House	25
George Street North	28
Wynyard Square	32
Bridge Street	36
Macquarie Street	41
Around Hyde Park	58
Hunter Street	74
Pitt Street	78
Pitt and Market Streets	83
Around Martin Plaza	91
Castlereagh Street	100
King Street	108
George Street	112
The Haymarket	122
Darling Harbour	128
Railway Square	132

Abbreviations used in this book:
ML - Mitchell Library
SPF - Small Picture File
SLNSW - State Library of New South Wales
GPO - Government Printing Office

Introduction

Pitt Street is remarkable for its neatness and cheerful appearance displayed by most of the cottages with which it is lined on either side; the small garden plots before them, their shaded verandahs ... have a direct tendency to recall the rustic beauties of Old England.

James Maclehose's romantic picture of the southern end of Pitt Street in 1839 reads like a fairy-tale when one looks at the street today. The cottages and those who lived in them have long vanished and multi-storey monoliths, occupied by another, quite different generation, stand in their place. The never ending process of change is happening before our eyes for sights and sounds, like ideas and values, come and go with the seasons. We have only to momentarily turn our backs when some fragment of our city - a familiar building, a theatre, a friendly store we associate with our own past - has been replaced. No wonder some of us seek the assurance of old places and old things.

The streets of that other Sydney, the Sydney of yesterday, casting a ghostly shadow behind today's concrete valleys and clashing traffic, are preserved in words and memories, photographs and engravings. I have selected some of these to present a portrait of the places and of the people who once populated the city of Sydney.

Alan Sharpe

The Dispossessed

The complex social structure sustained over thousands of years gave the indigenous people a sense of security seldom matched in the European experience. Occasional forays with rival tribes broke the tranquillity of their existence but hostility ceased as abruptly as it started. The people were at one with the land which provided spiritual and economic sustenance and when they partook of its natural offering these born conservationists moved on allowing the environment time to replenish.

They possessed nothing and wanted nothing. They made no improvements to the land neither did they exploit it. They roamed within their domain in groups of up to fifty sometimes meeting with other clans. 'From what I have seen of the natives of New-Holland,' wrote Captain James Cook, during his brief stay 18 years earlier. 'They may appear to be the most wretched people upon earth but in reality they are far more happier than we Europeans.'

Initially the Aborigines, believing the white trespassers to be returned spirits of their ancestors, regarded them with caution and curiosity treating them with courtesy for the Cadrigal tribe, occupying the area between Port Jackson and Botany Bay, were by and large a gentle people.

Governor Phillip and the military were anxious to establish friendly relations with the indigenous people and in succeeding years governors were inclined to give them preferential treatment over the convicts. Yet in spite of attempts at understanding, particularly by First Fleet men of goodwill, like marine Captain Watkin Tench, Judge Advocate David Collins and Lieutenant William Dawes, who failed to comprehend the fatal impact of eighteenth century European culture on this primitive society.

The spread of land tenure to emancipated convicts and the military lower ranks resulted in the first armed clashes as the Aborigines found themselves increasingly barred from land and river banks which had nourished them since the Dreamtime.

Fifteen months after the first landing the bodies of hundreds of natives were being discovered in coves, inlets and forests around Port Jackson. Devastating smallpox decimated not only the Cadrigals but also the Camaraigal tribe occupying the north shore, its infection extending to the Broken Bay tribe all of whom shared the Dharuk language.

Smallpox has been blamed on the First Fleet, although no cases were reported. The French scientific expedition, camped at Botany Bay days after Governor Phillip led his fleet around to Port Jackson, may have been responsible. Today it is suspected the deadly virus had visited upon the population before the arrival of the Europeans.

Among its victims was a young Aboriginal man named Arabanoo. A year after landing Governor Phillip sought an intermediary with the native population in a experiment typifying the man and his time. He had one of the natives kidnapped and brought to the settlement where he was treated with great kindness. At first Arabanoo failed to appreciate his loss of freedom but soon became adjusted enough to roam the settlement at will. The experiment was a failure and six months later he was dead of smallpox. Later Phillip was more successful in his choice of Bennelong, an Aboriginal with a sense of humour who soon adapted to the white man's tastes, especially in grog. Phillip even had a house built for him on a Point in Port Jackson which today bears his name.

Bennelong accompanied Governor Phillip to England, where he soon became homesick. He was never the same after he returned to Sydney.

Joseph Lycett's sweeping view of Sydney Heads in October 1824.
(Rex Nan Kivell Collection, National Library of Australia)

Strangers in the Forest

*I*t takes a vivid imagination to picture the place we call Circular Quay as it appeared more than 200 years ago. If we were to travel 35 kilometres north along the coast to explore the unspoiled foreshores of Broken Bay we may find a sheltered cove where a freshwater stream spills from the undergrowth out to the mud flats. Such a scene was witnessed from the crowded wooden decks of the vessels that dropped anchor on a hot January day in 1788. This pristine place was about to experience the shock of change for the newcomers were about to impose their will on the land.

So much to be done: storehouses for the precious provisions, a makeshift hospital, Governor Phillip's portable house to be erected. Sustenance and shelter were the first considerations: matters of the mind and needs of the soul took second place to discipline and order among this ill-matched gallery of men and women.

The settlement's progress was painfully slow. Not until the administration of the fourth governor, William Bligh, was a township clearly defined. A windmill turned on the western ridge where officers built their thatched cottages. Rough dwellings edged inland along the banks of the Tank Stream - to the east of which cultivated gardens reached up to Government House.

Possession. The British Flag flies at Sydney Cove. Governor Phillip's instructions from London regarding the 'natives' were clear. 'You are to endeavour ... to conciliate their affections, enjoining all our subjects to live in amity and kindness with them.' Should 'any of our subjects' harm them 'it is our will and pleasure that you do cause such offenders to be brought to punishment according to the degree of the offence'. (SPF, ML, SLNSW)

From the moment Governor Lachlan Macquarie came ashore in December 1809, development of the tiny colony, stagnating in apathy and antipathy, lurched forward. Street names were handed out, a market place established, roadwork pushed ahead. Aided by convict architect, Francis Greenway, Macquarie planned a series of buildings which eventually brought some dignity and cohesion to the township.

'Extravagant' was the verdict of Commissioner John Bigge on many of Macquarie's achievements. Bigge, sent by the Colonial Office to report on the administration, also considered the Governor's tolerance towards the convict population ill-advised. Yet, in spite of Commissioner Bigge, Macquarie managed to push many of his projects through. The Governor, embittered by the disregard for his achievements, departed for Scotland in February 1822 leaving his stamp firmly on the settlement he hoped would one day be a city.

The Precious Stream

The site on which Sydney was born was chosen because of a freshwater stream 'that stole silently through a very thick wood' out into the cove. Its source was the marshy acres of today's Hyde Park, between Market and Park Streets. From here water filtered over sandstone rock and down through tangled undergrowth to swell the rivulet which followed a course roughly parallel to Pitt Street.

The precious stream was vital to the new arrivals and Governor Phillip ensured no sun-filtering tree within 50 feet of its banks was to be removed. In that first year a convict work gang threw a log footbridge across the head of the stream linking the two halves of the settlement and giving Bridge Street its name. Governor King replaced it with a stone bridge 15 years later.

The Tank Stream divided the settlement in two: convict tents and marine barracks on the west bank; officers' quarters and administration on the east. On the ridge above, the Governor's house had a commanding view of the Harbour.

During the parched summer of 1790 Phillip had three tanks hacked out of the sandstone banks giving the Tank Stream its name. Five years later Governor Hunter issued an order forbidding its pollution as the water was used to wash clothes, clean fish and even, it was said, to empty chamber pots. Fences were later erected to protect the stream from straying cattle. In 1820 the *Sydney Gazette* admonished its readers:

With much pain we have lately observed individuals washing themselves in this stream of water, particularly in that part that runs centrally from King Street because that spot is almost secluded from every eye, that of curiosity accepted [sic].

As the importance of the stream declined, the quality of its waters degenerated until it was no longer useable. Townspeople then depended on private wells or costly water hauled by water carts from the Lachlan Swamps - long before they were dredged to form Centennial Park - until a tunnel from the swamp was completed in 1837.

In 1860 the unsavoury Tank Stream began to disappear from view when the stretch from Hunter Street to Bridge Street was built over. Eventually pipes carried the water from Bridge Street to Circular Quay and the last of the Tank Stream valley was filled in. Out of sight, it was soon forgotten until torrential rain flooded basements along Pitt Street.

Today the Tank Stream is carried by giant concrete pipes well beneath street level. Some of the tunnels are accessible for inspection and in the 1980s the Tank Stream was classified by the National Trust in recognition of its early significance to the city of Sydney.

The Tank Stream from a watercolour by Frederick Garling, 1842. The path on the right became Pitt Street and the house on the right was built by the rich emancipist Simeon Lord in 1804 and was known as Tank Stream House. (ML, SLNSW)

The Colony's Larder

The threat of famine hovered over the early years of settlement placing huge responsibility on the Commissary whose job was to regulate supplies of food, clothing and other necessities. John Palmer, former purser on Governor Phillip's flagship *Sirius*, was appointed in 1791. The charismatic Commissary won the confidence of a succession of governors and was granted 100 acres at the head of Garden Island Cove establishing Woolloomooloo Farm where he entertained in high style among his orchards and gardens.

Palmer's allegiance to Governor Bligh alienated him with the rebel administration and he was sentenced to three months gaol for distributing a proclamation issued by the deposed Governor. Palmer was reinstated by Governor Macquarie and appeared as a witness for Bligh at the trial of Colonel Johnston, the NSW Corps commandant, in England.

Palmer returned to Sydney in 1814 to find himself close to bankruptcy. His property was eventually sold.

'Little Jack' Palmer ended his days farming near Parramatta. When he died in September 1833 he was the last surviving officer of the First Fleet.

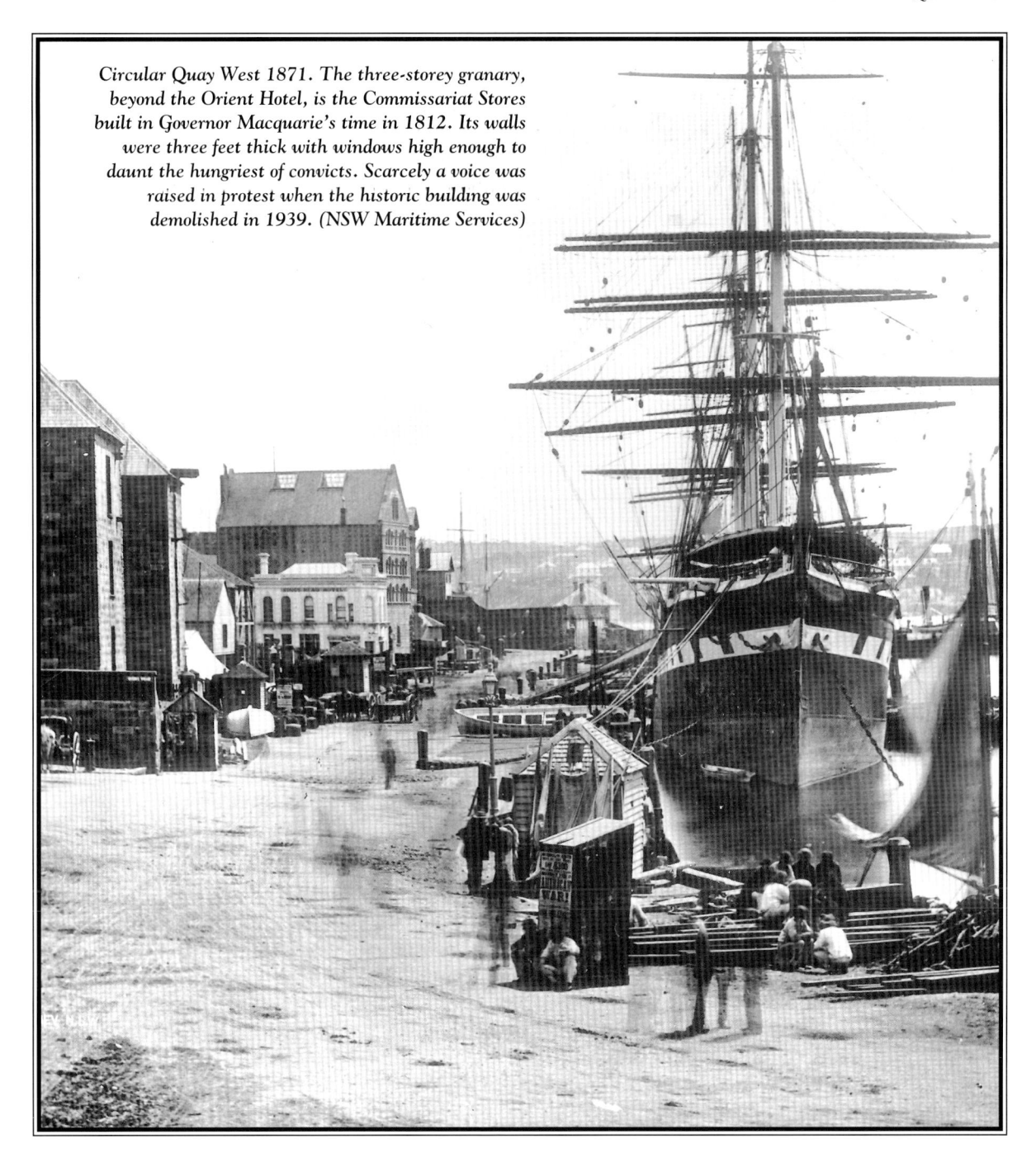

Circular Quay West 1871. The three-storey granary, beyond the Orient Hotel, is the Commissariat Stores built in Governor Macquarie's time in 1812. Its walls were three feet thick with windows high enough to daunt the hungriest of convicts. Scarcely a voice was raised in protest when the historic building was demolished in 1939. (NSW Maritime Services)

'King of the Wharf'

Among the grasping opportunists and greedy military clique who lorded over the infant colony there came a man of foresight and integrity: a tall young Scot named Robert Campbell. Campbell was a partner in the family trading company in Calcutta who arrived in Sydney to investigate trade prospects in 1798. He was 29 and, recognising the raw colony's potential, decided to stay.

He acquired a house on the west side of Sydney Cove and built a stone warehouse with a private wharf and an elegant house where the Overseas Passenger Terminal would one day be built. Officers of the NSW Corps resented the newcomer who threatened their immensely profitable trade in spirits but Campbell would not be intimidated.

He proceeded to break another monopoly. The august East India Company controlled all imports to England from the east but in 1805 Campbell sailed up the Thames with a shipment of fish oil and seal skins, in contravention of the rights of that company. His ship was seized and a legal wrangle followed in which Campbell won the day. This opened the door to free exports to England from the odd little colony on the other side of the globe.

As Robert Campbell's wealth and influence grew, his sympathies were with the embattled settlers and in 1805 he received a memorial on behalf of 200 settlers including the words: 'But for you we had still been a prey to the Mercenary unsparing Hand of Avarice and Extortion.'

Bligh's sympathies lay in the same direction as Campbell's and the Governor made the 'gentleman-like merchant' Colonial Treasurer and Port Naval Officer. In this capacity Campbell impounded a spirit still illegally imported by John Macarthur. It set in motion events leading to the 'Rum Rebellion' and the deposing of Bligh. Campbell and his wife were dining at Government House that summer evening when word came that Lieutenant-Colonel George Johnston and the NSW Corps were marching up Bridge Street to arrest the Governor.

As a key witness for Bligh, Campbell reluctantly left for England to appear at Johnston's trial. After five years absence he returned to Sydney to find himself close to bankruptcy forcing him to mortgage his elegant house, with its handsome furniture and paintings. It took ten years to regain his wealth with the support of Lachlan Macquarie whose wife's maiden name was Campbell.

In 1876 the Campbell property, including the house and garden, the warehouses and wharf, were sold to the Australasian Union Steamship Navigation Company who demolished the mansion in 1884.

The property was later sold to the government. Duntroon, the country property, remained in the possession of the Campbell family until 1910 when the Commonwealth Government acquired the homestead for use as a military college.

Campbell's Wharf and stores on the west side of Sydney Cove in the 1870s. (Public Transport Commission of NSW)

Cadman's Cottage

Cadman's Cottage is the oldest surviving dwelling in the Sydney city area. The two-storey, stone building below George Street North was built in 1816 to accommodate coxswain and crew of the government boats. Convict architect Francis Greenway was probably involved in its construction.

John Cadman, the fourth coxswain to occupy the cottage, was its longest tenant, residing there with his wife and two stepdaughters for 18 years from 1827 when Harbour tides washed over the sands fronting the cottage.

Cadman, a short, wiry man who had been sentenced to transportation for life for horse stealing, was 25 when he arrived in Sydney in May 1798. Eventually receiving a conditional pardon, he was listed as Assistant Government Coxswain in 1814.

In January 1827, Governor Darling made the conscientious Cadman Superintendent of the Government Boats, a post he held till 1845 when he received a retirement gratuity of £182. He and his wife bought a run-down licensed bar in George Street, Parramatta, and converted it into the Steam Packet Inn.

Cadman died in 1848 and was buried in the Devonshire Street Cemetery. His wife, Elizabeth, lived in Waverley during the 1850s and conducted the Harbour swimming baths in Manly a few years before her death in May 1861.

Cadman's Cottage was occupied by the water police until the Water Police Court was built on the corner of Albert and Phillip Street, Circular Quay in 1853. The cottage was restored as a residence for superintendents of the neighbouring Sailors' Home founded in 1863. In 1926 it was used as an overflow dormitory for the Home.

The old dwelling was left empty and decaying behind a corrugated iron fence for more than 25 years. In 1971 the Sydney Cove Redevelopment Scheme made provisions for the complete restoration of the cottage. Work began in October 1972 and a year later Cadman's Cottage opened to the public under supervision of the NSW National Parks and Wildlife Service.

During excavation of the basement in 1988 whisky bottles, ceramics, bones and pipe stems were uncovered. Further excavation in the 1990s exposed one of Sydney's first stormwater drains indicating the original shoreline.

Sydney Cove west six years before Cadman's Cottage was built in 1816.

The Quay Goes Full Circle

The construction of a quay across the mud flats at the mouth of the Tank Stream meant surrendering land occupied by Government House grounds so it waited.

One plan was to extend the south-to-north streets of Phillip, Elizabeth and Castlereagh down to the cove but public concern over costs prevented it. Only Pitt Street made it.

Hundreds of chained convicts toiled under the supervision of Colonial Engineer George Barney in reclaiming ten acres of tidal mudflats. It would be Sydney's last great convict-built enterprise. By 1844 Semi-Circular Quay, as it was called, curved round the east side of the cove to the mouth of the Tank Stream.

Despite the new quay pedestrians had to navigate the muddy flats of the Tank Stream to reach the west arm of the cove. It meant walking up to the Bridge Street bridge, crossing over and returning back down George Street. Some enterprising individuals built a 60-feet long footbridge from the new quay to George Street and called it the Halfpenny Bridge, the price of the toll.

By the 1850s gold discoveries and the sharp increase in wool multiplied shipping activity and the NSW Legislative Council decided to extend the Quay. When completed in 1855 Circular Quay buried the Tank Stream.

The quay goes full circle. (Illustrated Sydney News).

Circular Quay looking up Phillip Street in November 1870. The building in the middle is Thomas Mort's wool store with the Water Police Court standing opposite. Belmore's family hotel is visible and the little boy is standing in the vicinity of today's apartment building nicknamed the Toaster. (SPF, ML, SLNSW)

The Customs Officer and Customs House

Shipping activity was increasing in 1813 and a former captain in the NSW Corps was appointed Port Naval Officer. In collecting customs excise on spirits he was allowed 5 per cent in lieu of salary. The arrangement brought John Piper, 40, the princely income of £4 000 a year.

Piper arrived years earlier as a junior ensign and quickly rose through the ranks. A close friend of John Macarthur, he was, fortunately, serving on Norfolk Island during the rebellion against Governor Bligh. On Norfolk Island he formed a relationship with the 15-year-old daughter of a convict. He sailed for England with his de facto wife and children where he resigned from the regiment and returned to Macquarie's Sydney to take up his civilian post.

Piper's fortune advanced rapidly. He was granted 190 acres at Eliza Point, which became Point Piper, where he built his splendid Henrietta Villa for £10 000. Guests were entertained on the spacious verandas with extensive Harbour views or danced quadrilles far into the night. He added land at Vaucluse, Rose Bay, Woollahra and other locations around Sydney to his fortune. His several prestigious appointments included chairmanship of the Bank of NSW.

Gregarious and generous, if somewhat naive, the popular Piper's extravagant lifestyle got him in debt. Following Governor Darling's investigation into the affairs of the Bank of NSW, a deficiency of £12 000 was uncovered: the result of carelessness rather than corruption. Piper tried to drown himself but was saved. His properties were sold at a time when the market was down but his debt to the government and to his creditors was paid in full. Piper retired to a property in Bathurst and lived the life of a farmer-squire but was further impoverished by the rural depression of the early 1840s. Friends resettled his family on another property.

The first Customs House, completed in April 1845, was less colourful than its early officer had been. The current Collector of Customs, Colonel John Gibbes, urged a reluctant Governor Gipps to build a decent Customs House. The money finally came from London and Gipps turned its construction into an unemployment relief operation. The simple and sombre two-storey structure was devised by the Colonial Architect Mortimer Lewis and for a time the Customs Officer lived in a humble cottage next door.

In 1885 a classic-Revival style building, incorporating the front wall of the original building, was constructed on the site. Additions were made at the turn of the century and in 1916-17 a six-storey extension was added on top. The floor tiles in the new building featured the ancient swastika design, which created some controversy during World War II. The area in front of the Customs House was occupied for many years by market stalls 'in the manner of Whitechapel' and in the 1920s the City Council was collecting £10 000 a year from barrow owners. In the late 1990s the stately building, under the jurisdiction of the City Council, underwent a multi-million dollar restoration.

This is how Circular Quay looked to the returned men of the first AIF in 1919. Customs House is on the left. (Public Transport Commission of NSW)

The rebuilt Customs House in the 1880s. Although renovated and refurbished today it is partly obscured by the eyesore that is the Cahill Expressway. (GPO, ML, SLNSW)

Convict Tourist Ship

The former prison hulk Success was a popular exhibit around Australia in the 1890s. (National Library of Australia)

She sailed into Sydney with considerable fanfare in 1891, a floating prison museum promoted as 'the oldest ship in the world'. The posters promised a surviving relic from the days of convict transportation. Actually the 621-ton *Success* was built in Burma in 1840, one year before transportation to New South Wales ceased. She began life as an immigrant vessel arriving at Fremantle in 1843. Later she carried prospectors eagerly heading for the Victorian goldfields.

The Victorian Government purchased the *Success* and she became one of four prison hulks, tied up at Williamstown in 1853 to take the overflow from Melbourne's crowded gaols.

After serving as a store ship on the River Yarra she was purchased by a group of entrepreneurs for use as a prison show boat fitted out with cells, leg-irons, handcuffs and dummy figures in convict garb. She visited various ports around Australia and was put on show the same way historic replicas are displayed at Sydney's Maritime Museum today.

In 1894 the *Success* was displayed in ports around Britain. In 1912 she crossed the Atlantic to the USA where she received crowds of curious visitors wherever she called. During World War I the sailing ship was used as a cargo carrier before continuing her show tours after the war. She received considerable attention when exhibited at the Chicago World Fair in 1933. The *Success* was accidentally destroyed by fire in 1946.

The Water Police Court

An air of antiquity hangs over the small sandstone building that kneels at the foot of Phillip Street. It dates from 1853 but its classic revival style, designed by Edmund Blacket, makes it seem older. It was built to house the water police who controlled shipping and enforced Harbour regulations at a time of dramatic increase in shipping tonnage due to the gold discoveries. The building has been patched up ever since.

In 1885 an extension was added at the rear by the Colonial Architect, James Barnet, who attempted to integrate the two buildings by aligning the eaves. Fortunately its handsome arched portico is still recognisable

For many years the building held only two cells and those squeezed inside complained it rivalled the Black Hole of Calcutta. Prisoners were herded into a steel pen awaiting their appearance before the magistrate. A reporter in the late 1880s described some of the criminal types as having 'low foreheads, misplaced ears, full eyes, protruding under lips, square determined chins and badly-shaped heads with either too much or too little back to them'.

The Water Police Court (completed 1856) was the building to the left of the photograph, and the two storey building to the right was the Water Police Station. The 1886 addition designed by James Barnet was built in between the two buildings, where the white fence stands. The complex is now the Justice and Police Museum. It is open to the public on weekends and is managed by Historic Houses Trust of NSW. (GPO, ML, SLNSW)

Circular Quay

Horse buses and hansom cabs dominated Sydney streets. The two centres were the rail terminus (today's Central Station) and Circular Quay, seen here in the early 1880s, before the trams took over and the Sydney sprawl began.

Circular Quay in the first half of the 20th century, before the Cahill Expressway opened in 1958 and the high rise took off in the 1960s. In the foreground is the Mariner's Church, built in 1856. The pulpit takes the form of a ship's prow.

The Rocks

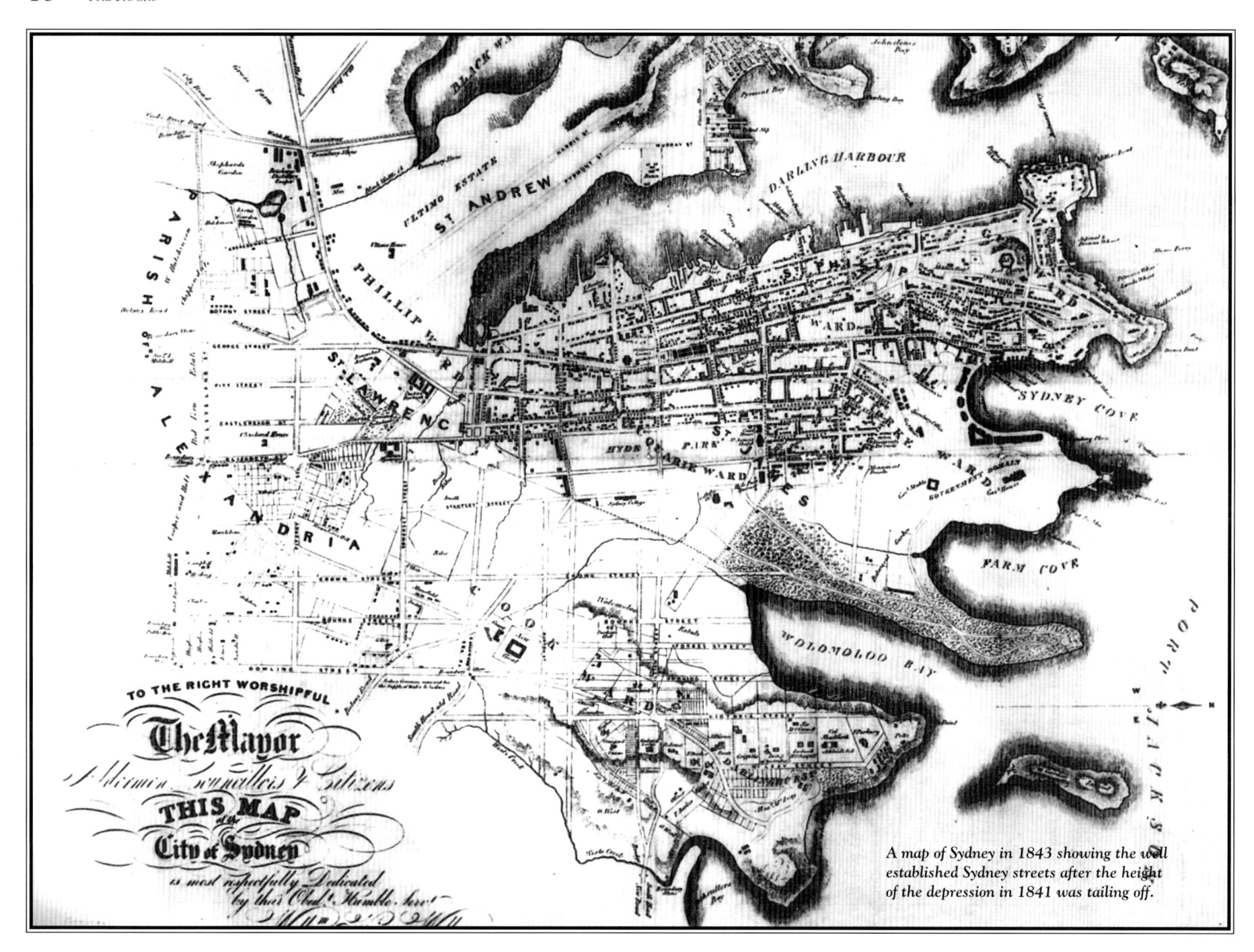

A map of Sydney in 1843 showing the well established Sydney streets after the height of the depression in 1841 was tailing off.

Back to The Rocks

A scatter of timber shanties occupied the slopes west of Sydney Cove. Those homes below the winding tracks were subjected to sewerage and drainage from backyards above. Access to The Rocks was gained by steep flights of steps, ideal cover for nightly assaults on lone seamen heading up to the brothels and grog shops.

In 1843 a party of chained convicts began the huge task of hacking through solid rock to provide a road from Millers Point to the Cove. The tools were inadequate and the project eventually abandoned. Sixteen years later, when Sydney had become an expanding city, the rock was finally driven through by free labour and the help of explosives, to form the Argyle Cut.

In 1858 William Jevons, a keen observer of Sydney social life, found many of the women living in the area wore 'dirty clothes' having 'slovenly manners and repulsive countenances'.

'I am acquainted with some of the worse parts of London … and some unhealthy parts of Liverpool, Paris and other towns but nowhere have I seen such a retreat of filth and vice as The Rocks.'

As the century progressed, people with money, attracted by the splendid views, Harbour breezes and the proximity to town, built two-storey brick houses on the upper slopes.

By the 1870s a colony of Chinese settlers crowded into the area around Lower George Street, sometimes with ten to a room. Resentment towards 'Johnny Pigtail' by the locals resulted in the Chinese shifting to the Campbell Street market area.

Elliot Johnson's pencil drawing catches the archaic character of The Rocks with its stone terraces and worn stairs. Johnson arrived as a seaman in 1883 and may have stayed at the unsavoury Ocean Wave Hotel. He remained to become a federal parliamentarian and received a knighthood in 1920.

Gloucester Street looking north from Essex Street at the turn of the century. The houses on the left could date from the 1840s. Note the baby in the pram.
(State Archive of NSW)

When work began on the southern approaches to the Harbour Bridge in 1926, the impact on The Rocks was devastating. Some 300 homes were demolished and families who had lived there for generations moved to other parts of Sydney. The main thoroughfare, Princes Street, disappeared altogether.

In 1968 the Sydney Cove Development Authority was given the task of revitalising the area. What remained of The Rocks was preserved and historic buildings were restored to their original prominence which recreated some of the atmosphere of the past. Fortunately the community woke up to the historic significance of The Rocks just in time.

Plague and Fire

The bubonic plague ravaged a corner of Sydney in 1900. Fleas living on infected rats spread the epidemic as it had done in Europe during the Black Plague in the 14th century. Contamination centred on the wharf area, Millers Point and The Rocks. Between January and August, 303 city dwellers contracted the disease and 103 people died.

The council took draconian measures: streets were blocked off and a bounty placed on the number of rats caught. Hundreds of suspect premises were incinerated. Some isolated cases turned up in the Eastern Suburbs and a number of people fled to the Blue Mountains. The plague subsided by the end of the year.

Even rat catchers employed to clean up the infested Rocks area were shocked by the 'many sad cases of poverty'.
(State Archives of NSW)

The Argyle Cut

It was one of the great engineering feats of early Sydney, it also brought recognition to the disreputable Rocks. The work was started in 1843 by convict chain gangs shuffling down from Hyde Park Barracks clutching their inadequate picks and hammers. The plan was to extend Argyle Street by hacking through a huge rock mass opening the road from the northern end of Kent Street to the warehouses and wharfs in George Street, thus providing a direct route from Darling Harbour.

The chief overseer was Tim Lane a man with a grim wit who encouraged his charges with the promise that 'by the help of God and the strong arm of the flogger, you'll get fifty before breakfast tomorrow!' Even with such words of 'encouragement' he and his convict labourers were unable to break through and the project was abandoned. Some years later with the use of free labour and new types of explosives, the job was punched through and the two halves of Argyle Street were finally joined.

The bridge carrying Cumberland Street across the Cut was finished in 1864 and four years later a second bridge linked the north and south ends of Princes Street which, like other streets in the area, disappeared during the Harbour Bridge reclamations.

The Rocks from the eastern side of Circular Quay in 1870, taken from the grounds of Government House, looking towards Dawes Point, seen on the right. Campbell's old wool stores accommodate tourist facilities today. (SPF, ML, SLNSW)

A barefoot boy takes advantage of The Cut in 1901. Today the Argyle Visitors Centre is a mecca for tourists. (National Library of Australia)

Green Ban Man

In June 1971 the NSW Builders' Labourers Federation supported residents of suburban Hunters Hill by placing a ban on the development of environmentally sensitive Kellys Bush. Secretary Jack Mundey called it a 'green ban.' In November an industrial ban was imposed on the commercial development of The Rocks.

Three years later the builders' labourers joined The Rocks' action groups in a fiery demonstration against demolition of Sydney's most historic precinct. Demonstrators,

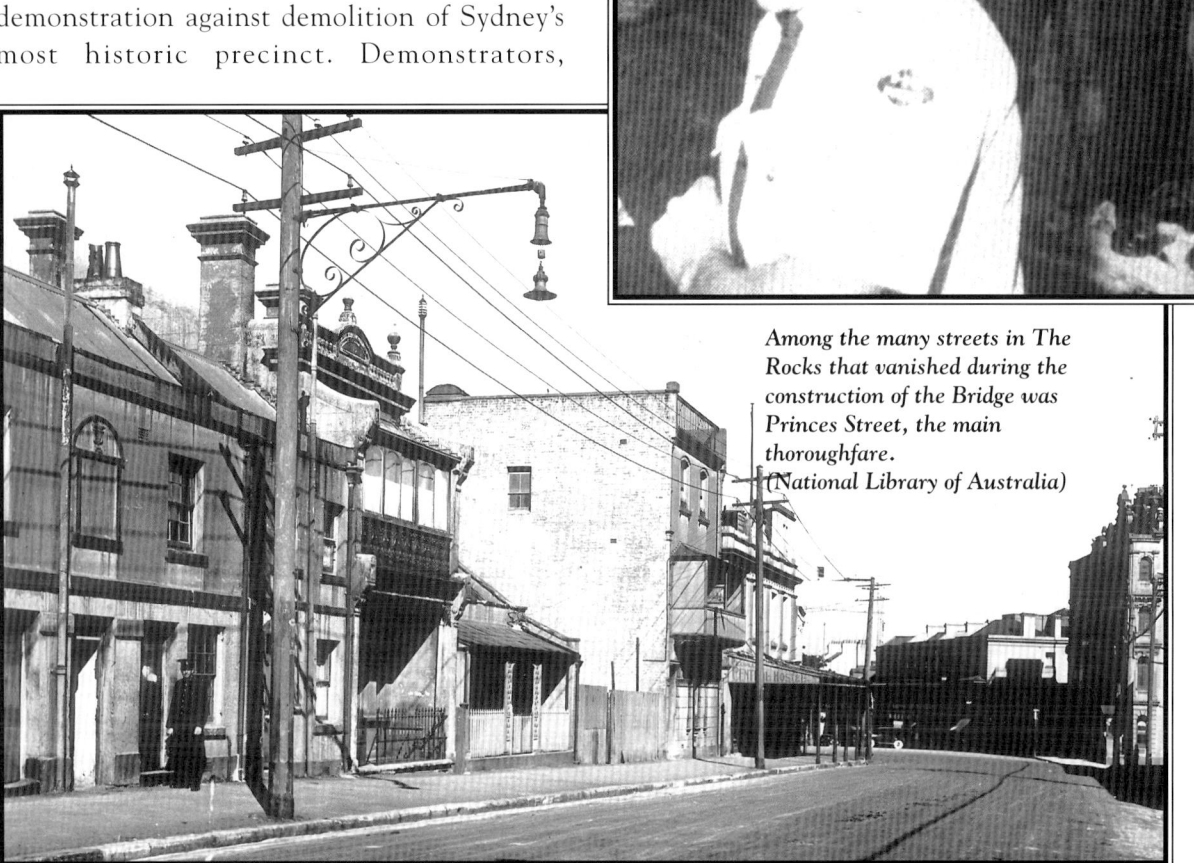

Among the many streets in The Rocks that vanished during the construction of the Bridge was Princes Street, the main thoroughfare. (National Library of Australia)

Jack Mundey being arrested during a protest at the demolition of the Playfair Building at the Rocks in 1973. The term 'green ban' was coined by Mundey. The BLF saved residential areas in The Rocks, Woolloomooloo, and also parts of Moore Park, Centennial Park and the Botanic Gardens. (News Limited)

barricaded in partly-demolished houses, fought the police, four of whom were injured. More than 70 people were arrested including Mundey who became hero of the hour. Thanks to Mundey and his socially conscious men, The Rocks is now a major Sydney tourist attraction.

In the 2000 Australia Day Honours List Jack Mundey belatedly received the Order of Australia.

The Triumphant Arch

In a modest ceremony at North Sydney 28 July 1923 a round of applause sounded as a spade sank into the earth. Five years after World War I the turning of the sod marked the start of the Sydney Harbour Bridge. When the Bridge's opening ceremony took place almost nine years later the country was overwhelmed by the Depression and the Bridge would stand as evidence of the people's abiding faith in their nation's future.

Architect of the great engineering feat was Dr J.J.C.Bradfield, Chief Engineer of Sydney Harbour, whose skill and enthusiasm saw the construction carried to its finality. His attention to every detail provided tenderers with materials to be used with the exact cost and the Yorkshire firm of Dorman, Long & Co. Ltd got the job.

Sydneysiders keenly observed progress and, as the day approached to link the two arms of the arch, bets were taken as to whether they would meet exactly in the middle. At 4.15 pm, 19 August 1930 they joined perfectly, ferry passengers cheered and workers got two shillings each to toast 'success to the bridge'.

In one of the final tests 72 locomotives steamed onto the Bridge buffer to buffer but the Bridge stood firm.

The opening on a sunny 19 March 1932 was a scene of pomp and pageantry witnessed by tens of thousands. An unexpected incident added drama to the occasion as Labour Premier Jack Lang was about to cut the ribbon when he was upstaged by a mounted army officer who galloped 'out of nowhere' and sliced the ribbon with his sword. His name was Captain (Ret.) Francis van de Groot a member of the New Guard (an extreme anti-communist organisation) which was bitterly opposed to Lang. De Groot was dragged off and eventually fined £5.

In July 1959 the removal of the tram lines on the eastern side of the Bridge added two more motor traffic lanes, easing some of the congestion for another decade but by the 1980s the traffic situation was close to desperate. It brought about the realisation of a century old dream: a tunnel beneath the Harbour.

The Sydney Harbour Tunnel opened to traffic on Saturday, 29 August 1992 giving motorists the choice of crossing under or over the Harbour.

On the fiftieth anniversary of the opening of the Bridge in 1982, traffic was barred and the public was allowed to stroll from one side to the other as they did on the first day.

The huge turnout surprised the organisers, the roadway becoming so jammed with people at one stage that there was fear for their safety. Fortunately good humour overcame the possibility of panic. The Bridge was also closed for the Corroboree March in May 2000. Today tourist parties can walk over the top of the arch.

The rigours of the riggers hovering over the Harbour glad to be employed on the Bridge when one quarter of the workforce was unemployed. (Henri Mallard Collection, The Australian Centre of Photography)

24 THE HARBOUR BRIDGE

Until the opening of the Harbour Bridge in 1932 scores of ferries fanned out from Circular Quay. Soon the great arch will join but will the ends meet?

The Evolution of Bennelong Point

The rock promontory on which the Sydney Opera House stands was the temporary home of cows and horses landed for Governor Phillip's farm. Named Bennelong Point, after the Aboriginal befriended by Governor Phillip, a storehouse was erected there. Two brass cannons were in place before being moved across to Dawes Point. When a convict escaped or someone was lost in the bush, the guns boomed a signal across the Harbour.

In December 1817 Governor Macquarie laid the foundation stone for 'a neat, handsome fort' that would bear his name. Constructed by convict labour in two years it became a picturesque landmark for visiting ships.

Fort Macquarie was built within four square walls initially entered by a drawbridge. The fort contained ten 24-pounder cannon and five 6-pounders. A two-storey stone tower provided living quarters for one officer and 12 artillerymen.

Following the outbreak of the Crimean War the colony became acutely defence conscious and £10 000 was voted for Harbour defences to provide more cannons for the fort.

News of the Franco-Prussian War, although remote from Sydney resulted in more cannon and more artillerymen being seconded to the fort. The cannons only sounded on vice-regal occasions or to salute the arrival of an important vessel.

The removal of the fort's sea wall in 1890 was part of wharf improvements. The life of the old fort was drawing to a close and the guns that celebrated the accession of Queen Victoria, the fall of Sebastopol and the arrival of a succession of governors were silenced forever.

Macquarie's fort was demolished in 1903 and replaced by a tram terminal with a fortress-like design. It remained in service until the last Sydney tram disappeared from the streets in February 1961 when it was demolished to make way for the Opera House. Trams known as 'street rail' have returned to the southern end of the city.

A phony fort for trams replaced a real fort for troopers in 1903.

'Absolutely Breathtaking'

The year was 1957, the 'postwar period' was over, full employment reigned, the migration program was putting the gloss on a growing population and the country was buoyant with self-confidence. A strong streak of conservatism persisted in the face of which courage and imagination triumphed when a daring design for an Opera House was accepted.

The courtly Sir Eugene Goossens, who in ten years whipped the Sydney Symphony into a world-class orchestra, convinced NSW Labor Premier, Joe Cahill, it was time Sydney had a grand opera house. The international design competition was won at the last minute by 38-year-old Danish architect Joern Utzon. He had never visited Australia and when he arrived, full of enthusiasm, he proclaimed the site 'absolutely breathtaking'.

The Opera House took 15 years to build. It was estimated to cost $7 million but finished up costing $102 million. Its progress was fraught with every imaginable setback: arguments, recriminations, strikes, soaring costs and bruised egos. It was the stick with which each Opposition beat the incumbent Government no matter which party ruled. It finally drove its designer back to Denmark half way through the project, never to return, not even for the opening, the building's completion left to a team of local architects.

Visiting music celebrities sneered at or applauded its design. Visiting writers and artists sought for metaphors to show their approval or disgust: 'A flight of doves', a 'string of Roman helmets,' 'hindquarters of a giant crayfish'. All seemed anxious to avoid likening it to what it represented: a set of billowing sails.

The Queen was invited to open the Opera House on 20 October 1973 and those 'sails' soon joined the Harbour Bridge in representing Sydney in the eyes of the world.

To stand on the terrace at night gazing across at the illuminated Sydney Harbour Bridge arching above the shadowy waters of the Harbour, is to feel the pulse of a great city in repose.

Danish architect Joern Utzon delighted by the location for the Opera House during his first visit to Sydney.
He is talking to Premier Joe Cahill. Photographed by Ken Renshaw on 29 July 1957 for the Australian Photographic Agency.
(ML, SLNSW)

On 20 October 1973, 15 000 invited guests, 2 000 small craft and the Queen withstood 70 kilometre an hour winds which quickly carried off 60 000 balloons. When the red streamers at the front of the building parted, the Opera House was officially 'launched'. Ben Blakeney, an Aboriginal actor, played a didgeridoo from the roof of the Concert Hall in memory of Bennelong and his people. Photographed by Jack Hickson, the Australian Photographic Agency. (SLNSW)

The Sydney Gaol

In June 1797 Governor Hunter built his 'exceedingly wanted' log gaol in George Street. It was 80 feet long with thatched roof and a clay floor and divided into 22 log cells.

In spite of the fire hazard, logs were used due to a shortage of bricks. A disgruntled incendiary did set it alight and Parramatta's log gaol went up in smoke ten months later in November 1799. The new stone gaol took two years to build. Hunter imposed a tax on landed spirits to pay for it.

He was proud of his 'handsome and commodious' prison with its 'six strong and secure cells for condemned felons' which stood behind a high wall in Lower George Street. Its southern wall ran up steep Essex Street where the gallows provided a spectacle for residents of The Rocks.

By the 1820s the Sydney Gaol was overflowing and in 1826 the disabled vessel *Phoenix* was commandeered for use as a prison hulk and was tied up in Lavender Bay.

Sydney had outgrown its beginnings as a penal settlement by the 1830s and was now a busy township. Its citizens found the gaol's presence, with the occasional body dangling from the gallows, an affront. Governor Bourke ordered his Colonial Architect to design a stone gaol out on Darlinghurst Hill.

In 1841 a pitiful procession of 119 men and 39 women trailed out of their fetid cells in George Street and shuffled with clinking irons through the streets of Sydney, followed by the catcalls of the populace, to their clean, new quarters on Darlinghurst Hill.

George Street north from the guardhouse on Grosvenor Street corner in 1826. The wall of the Male Orphan Asylum is opposite. The two-storey house belongs to James Underwood another merchant to ascend from convict to capitalist. The white wall down on the left surrounds the gaol. The Regent Hotel now occupies the site, its restaurant named after early gaoler Henry Kable.

A Garrison Town

Early nineteenth century Sydney was a garrison town; by the end of the century it had become a 'sailor type' city. Until the late 1840s a ten feet high, two feet thick stone wall ran along George Street cutting off the expanding commercial town centre from its military guardians. Within the walls were three double-storey blockhouses which made it one of the largest military barracks in the British Empire. It was supposed to protect the colony from enemy invasion but Governor Macquarie, who loved building walls, had it erected to 'restrain as much as possible intercourse between the military and the inhabitants of the town'.

The redcoats generally kept to themselves, crowding into corner taverns along Clarence (Middle Soldiers' Row until 1810) and Kent (Back Soldiers' Row) Streets where many lived in squalid cottages with their wives or mistresses and their children. To supplement their meagre pay some of the soldiers peddled cabbage tree hats to the populace.

For 60 years the flower of Britain's infantry regiments served in the Australian colonies beginning with the 73rd Highland Regiment, who arrived with Governor Macquarie, up until the departure of the last British troops in 1870. It was as if the Colonial Office was compensating for sending the notorious NSW Corps.

The barracks' wall began just north of present Margaret Street and extended to Barrack Street, the whole occupying the area between George and Clarence Streets. The blocks stood between York and Clarence Streets. There were gates on four sides of the walls, the main gate, with guardhouse, located in George Street close to the present Wynyard Station ramp. From here a wide gravel path, leading to the main building, was bordered by green lawns.

Officers usually associated themselves with the town's 'exclusives', families residing in the colony from choice. On one occasion junior officers of the 46th Regiment left the table en masse when the emancipist Dr William Redfern, the former naval surgeon transported for his part in the Nore mutiny, was invited into the mess.

In a tradition continued long after by the Royal Navy, a free tot of rum was issued to the troops at lunchtime. In 1845 Colonel Maurice O'Connell reduced the rum issue and the entire regiment refused to attend parade until it was given back. A furious O'Connell rashly ordered the 11th Regiment up from Tasmania to crush the 'mutiny'. By time the Hobart sailed into the Harbour and three hundred troopers marched up George Street in time to martial music, the Sydney garrison had returned to their duties and the arrivals were greeted with scornful cheers.

There were cheers from the civilian population in 1847 when the 11th North Devonshire Regiment marched out of the George Street Barracks for the last time to take up billets in the new Victoria Barracks. The arrangement was unpopular with the soldiers who preferred being stationed in town than among the remote sandhills of Paddington.

Between 1850 and 1853 the valuable land behind George Street was subdivided and sold. In October 1851 the public was invited to attend an auction of building materials from the dismantled barracks. Some were used for the shops and bank buildings that went up when the barrack walls came down.

The George Street Barracks' square became Wynyard Square.

George Street's Grave History

Sydney's early burial grounds were primitive arrangements set in paddocks on the edge of the settlement, and were carelessly built over as land values increased. In November 1788 a convict woman wrote of one location being 'at the extremity of the lines where since our arrival the dead are buried'. The 'lines' were four rows of convict tents in the area between Essex and Grosvenor Streets.

The increase in the number of burial grounds in a period of five years resulted from the soaring death rate following the arrival of the tragic Second Fleet in June 1790.

In 1847 when the army moved out of George Street Barracks - facing today's Wynyard Square - and took up residence in Paddington, the land was subdivided and coffins were dug up in the vicinity of Clarence and Margaret Streets.

In 1815 Market Street was the town's perimeter, and the cemetery was situated in the rustic outskirts, the site of the present Town Hall. It was in a sorry state for years. One visitor wrote: 'In wet weather the place is very offensive from the stench arising from the bodies some of which are not far underground.'

The George Street ground accommodated some 2000 bodies in 27 years. One of the oldest surviving tombstones, dated 20 June 1798, belonged to Captain Gavin Hamilton of the ill-fated Sydney Cove, Robert Campbell's vessel which sank while returning from Van Diemen's Land.

Sydney's population grew rapidly during Macquarie's governorship and sacred ground was set aside one mile west of the town. The first interment at the Sandhills Cemetery - later known as the Old Devonshire Street Ground - was in September 1819 when the coffin containing the remains of Quartermaster Hugh McDonald of the 46th regiment was lowered into the ground.

In the 1860s the historian James Bonwick was shocked at the neglected state of the defunct George Street cemetery: 'Graves were open in many cases and boys burrowing beneath. From the numerous cavities showing the old timber and the remains of brick vaults the stench was terrible. The places were used for common purposes of nature with a most revolting and disgusting disregard of decency.'

One of the oldest monuments Bonwick saw was that of First Fleet convict Jane Dundas who was a housemaid at Government House during Governor Arthur Phillip's time. When Governor King's wife visited England she took Jane with her. The two women returned to Sydney and Jane became housekeeper. When she died in December 1805, age 47, the King family lamented the loss of 'an honest, faithful and affectionate servant'.

In the mid-1970s when excavations for an underground shopping arcade were underway, several vaults were discovered at the site, one of which contained a coffin.

It is estimated that 5000 citizens of Sydney were buried in the Sandhills Cemetery from 1819 to 1868 when burials ceased. A number of pioneers, who names crop up in our history books, were interred in the Sandhills Cemetery, their bones mingling with those of executed thieves and murderers. The ground closed when the cemetery at Botany was consecrated.

The Old Devonshire Street Cemetery, as it was now called, was overgrown when the land was resumed for Central Station. The public was invited to relocate the remains of ancestors and in 1901 a procession of carts and steam trams were loaded with coffins and headstones and conveyed to Botany Cemetery and other suburban cemeteries for re-burial.

George Street about eight years after settlement as drawn by convict artist Thomas Watling. Soldiers can be seen far right outside timber barracks, later replaced by the brick George Street Barracks. The second row of cottages is Pitt Street; Hunter Street runs up the hill on the left.
(Mitchell Library)

St Phillip's Church

The first religious service was held 'under a great tree' on the second Sunday after the landing of the First Fleet. It was conducted by the Reverend Richard Johnson, an earnest young chaplain who wished he'd never come to the place. A church was low on Governor Phillip's list of priorities and Johnson had to make do with open-air services. During a visit by a Spanish man-o'-war, the ship's captain wryly observed if Spain had settled the colony, a House of God would be built before a House of Man.

Following Governor Phillip's departure Johnson built a church costing £67 which he paid out of his own pocket. The church, with wattle and daub (mud) walls and thatched roof, was T-shaped; the nave seated 500. It stood on the Hunter and Castlereagh Street (called Chapel Row) corner. An obelisk marks the spot. The first service was held in August 1793. Five years later the church was gutted by fire by 'some wicked and disaffected person' in protest against compulsory attendance.

In 1798 Governor Hunter laid the foundation for a new church to be called St Phillip's after the first Governor. King George III himself donated a fine service of silver communion plate. The sandstone church with a slate roof, incorporated two galleries, one exclusively for use by the military. The church took 12 years to complete.

St Phillip's opened on Christmas Day 1810 and the service was conducted by the Reverend William Cowper who had arrived the previous year. Shocked by the colony's lax morals he continually admonished the congregation. A few years later Cowper was struck down by gaol (rheumatic) fever that plagued him the rest of his life.

He was 63 when he was compelled to visit England for treatment of his failing eyesight. He returned to Sydney almost cured and saw his dream realised with the laying of the foundation for a new church behind the original small and dilapidated structure.

St Phillip's Church on 16 November 1865 with a clear view of the harbour.

Edmund Blacket designed the new church in the 'English Perpendicular Gothic' style and it was widely praised when it opened in March 1856. The original organ was replaced in 1875.

During his long association with St Phillip's, Cowper won the respect of a succession of governors. Governor Darling found him 'a very exemplary man'. Throughout his life in the colony Cowper studiously avoided becoming embroiled in church or political issues, determined 'neither willingly nor intentionally to offend anyone'. He received a state funeral when he died in 1858.

Looking down Margaret Street to George Street in the 1880s. Cohen's Hotel later became Pfahlert's Hotel and moved across the road when the old hotel was demolished in the late 1920s. Today the All Seasons Premier Menzies Hotel occupies part of the site. (SPF, ML, SLNSW)

An Old Colonial Hostelry

Many who remember the imposing white residence with broad verandas which gave a charming colonial touch to York Street, just north of Wynyard Square, may well marvel that the building remained intact so long. It was Petty's Hotel before it was sold to the Red Cross for use as a blood bank in 1950. Petty's was once the prince of Sydney hotels; the first choice of distinguished overseas visitors and favoured by squatters from 'up country'. Robert Louis Stevenson once turned up from Samoa in beachcomber attire and was turned away by the haughty hotel porter.

In 1828 the Reverend John Dunmore Lang acquired a cottage opposite his Scots' Church and built a manse. The fiery minister's pet project, the Australian College (which closed in Lang Street in 1854) brought him close to bankruptcy and he was forced to sell the manse to William Cummings who turned it into an 11 room hotel in 1833. Three years later another innkeeper, Thomas Petty, who owned Pulteneys Hotel in Bent Street, took over from Cummings and gave the hotel the name that lasted 114 years.

The hotel was refurbished and extensions added in 1850 turning it into the aristocrat of Sydney hotels where the food, served on silver plate in the gold and white dining room, was of the highest standard. In those days the hotel could boast sweeping views of the Harbour. An advertisement in the 1860s breathlessly described it 'nestled in a calm, quiet and sweet retreat in the heart of the surging city; with tall nodding palms throwing soft shade and delicious breezes over its wide verandahs'. In the mid-1880s a visitor who spent three months there, claimed 'I was never more comfortable anywhere. The situation is retired, quiet, and central. The original building is old and rambling, and the rooms are small; but the cuisine is excellent.'

Petty's heyday was the 1890s when it was said to be favoured by the 'travelled, cultured Australian' although innumerable paintings of horses and racing memorabilia suggested the interests of the proprietor and his patrons lay in another direction.

The old colonial hostelry was removed to make way for the towering Wynyard Travelodge. Today protests over the removal of a building of Petty's historic significance would be too resounding to ignore.

Petty's Hotel in York Street was taken over by the Red Cross Blood Bank in 1950. (SPF, ML, SLNSW)

WYNYARD SQUARE

The old barracks square became a dumping ground when the military moved out to Paddington in 1847. Happily it became Wynyard Park, a stretch of green in the CBD. It received it's name from Major-General E. B. Wynyard who was in command of the 58th Regiment.

York Street in 1871, beside Wynyard Square, was residential, sunny and relatively treeless. It was a short stroll to the Harbour or Sunday church at St Phillips. (National Library of Australia)

The First Government House

Long before Bridge Street was named it was distinguished by the presence of Government House. Governor Phillip's two-storey, buff brick and stone residence contained six rooms and the colony's first stairway. Here, on 4 June 1789, Governor Phillip and his guests toasted the birthday of King George III.

Successive governors complained of their accommodation each consoling himself by adding an extension. Their wives could scarce complain of the lovely view over shrubs and vegetable patches to the sparkling Harbour with the dark wooded hills of the north shore beyond. Governor Bligh's daughter, Mary Putland, helped landscape part of the four acre garden sloping to the waters' edge.

Governor Macquarie made many improvements including a dining room with a bay window. By the time the new Government House was built the old residence with its outbuildings, had grown haphazardly. The entire complex was unceremoniously demolished in 1845, opening Bridge Street to Macquarie Street.

Sydneysiders seemed determined to deny the site its special significance. It was occupied by small shops and a carrier's yard and for 20 years following World War I, a tin shed housed a public works department on the site.

In March 1899 workmen installing a telegraph tunnel uncovered a copper plate sandwiched between two stones. It proved to be the foundation stone for the first Government House which had been laid on 15 May 1788. The plate is now displayed in the Museum of Sydney.

In 1982 the NSW State Government gave its approval for the commercial development of the site then used as a car park. Its historic significance suddenly became news and a team of archaeologists uncovered the rear wall of the original house. The following year a rally was held in Macquarie Place in support of the site against 'the wanton intrusion of big business'. This time the government listened. Appropriately it is now the site of the Museum of Sydney.

The first Government House was the hub of the colony for 56 years. Each of the eight governors who resided there complained of its inconveniences. Today the Museum of Sydney occupies the site on the corner of Phillip and Bridge Streets.

Bligh's Other Mutiny

*I*t was 26 January 1808, the twentieth anniversary of the birth of Sydney. It was also the day Bridge Street sounded to the thump of military boots and the fife and drum strains of 'The British Grenadiers'. At nine in the evening the rank and file of the NSW Corps in scarlet tunics and black shako hats, bayonets fixed, wheeled left out of the barrack gates in George Street, tramped across the Tank Stream bridge and marched up the hill to Government House to arrest the 'tyrant' who tried to break the officers' rum monopoly: Governor William Bligh.

When the 52-year-old naval officer had arrived to take up the governorship 17 months earlier, Corps officers had already become the aristocracy. They controlled the import of spirits, especially rum, which had become a form of currency in the thirsty colony. Rum even paid for labour. Bligh was chosen as governor because he was 'Firm on discipline, civil in deportment, and not subject to whimper and whine, when severity of discipline is wanted.' He tackled the 'Rum Corps' monopoly head on, threatening heavy penalties for using spirits as a means of exchange.

Bligh's clash with John Macarthur, the manipulative officer behind the monopoly, was inevitable. It came to a head when Bligh ordered Macarthur's arrest for importing illicit spirit stills. When a court of six Corps officers refused to try their colleague, tense discussion and behind-the-scene intrigue culminated in the commanding officer, Lieutenant-Colonel George Johnston, leading the revolt against the Governor.

It was claimed that the doughty Bligh was found hiding under a bed - an unlikely circumstance for an officer who showed remarkable courage in the epic voyage in an open boat following the mutiny aboard the Bounty.

Bligh was confined in Sydney until he agreed to return to England. Instead he sailed to Hobart where the Lieutenant-Governor, David Collins, refused to help him regain office. Bligh returned to Sydney when Governor Macquarie arrived and lingered for several months, much to the Governor's annoyance. Recent history has been generous towards the former captain of Bounty. Bombastic and unbending he may have been but there is evidence he was neither excessively harsh nor deliberately cruel.

Johnston was tried in England three years later and cashiered from the army. He returned to the colony and retired to his property at Annandale with his ex-convict wife, the former Esther Abrahams.

Government House, January 1808. George Johnston proclaims the arrest of Governor Bligh. (Painting by Raymond Lindsay)

The Old 'change

In December 1851 the Royal Exchange, a four-storey sandstone building opened its doors on the corner of Bridge and Pitt Streets in a ceremony attended by the Governor, Sir William Denison. A highlight of that occasion was the inauguration of the first morse telegraph but the attempt to connect with the lookout post at South Head failed when word came back that the Governor's message was illegible.

The Royal Exchange was formed by a group of merchants to provide a common meeting place for bankers, shipping agents and businessmen to meet and talk and trade. In those days Sydney was desperately short of dignified venues - even inquests were held in hotels - and on certain evenings the buzz of male voices within the panelled walls of the Exchange gave way to the sweeter strains of the violin and bass fiddle at musical soirees.

In 1872 the Sydney Stock Exchange was inaugurated in the building and in 1880 Sydney's first telephone exchange was installed with a line connecting to the Darling Harbour woolshed. When the first public telephone line was installed the distinction went to the real estate agency Messrs. Richardson and Wrench.

The Royal Exchange became a landmark for visitors to Sydney and in the 1890s it was distinguished by the visit of two literary personalities: Joseph Conrad and Robert Louis Stevenson on a visit from Samoa.

By the mid-twentieth century the stately old building had long outlived its usefulness and wreckers tore it down to replace it with a 30 storey glass and concrete tower in 1967.

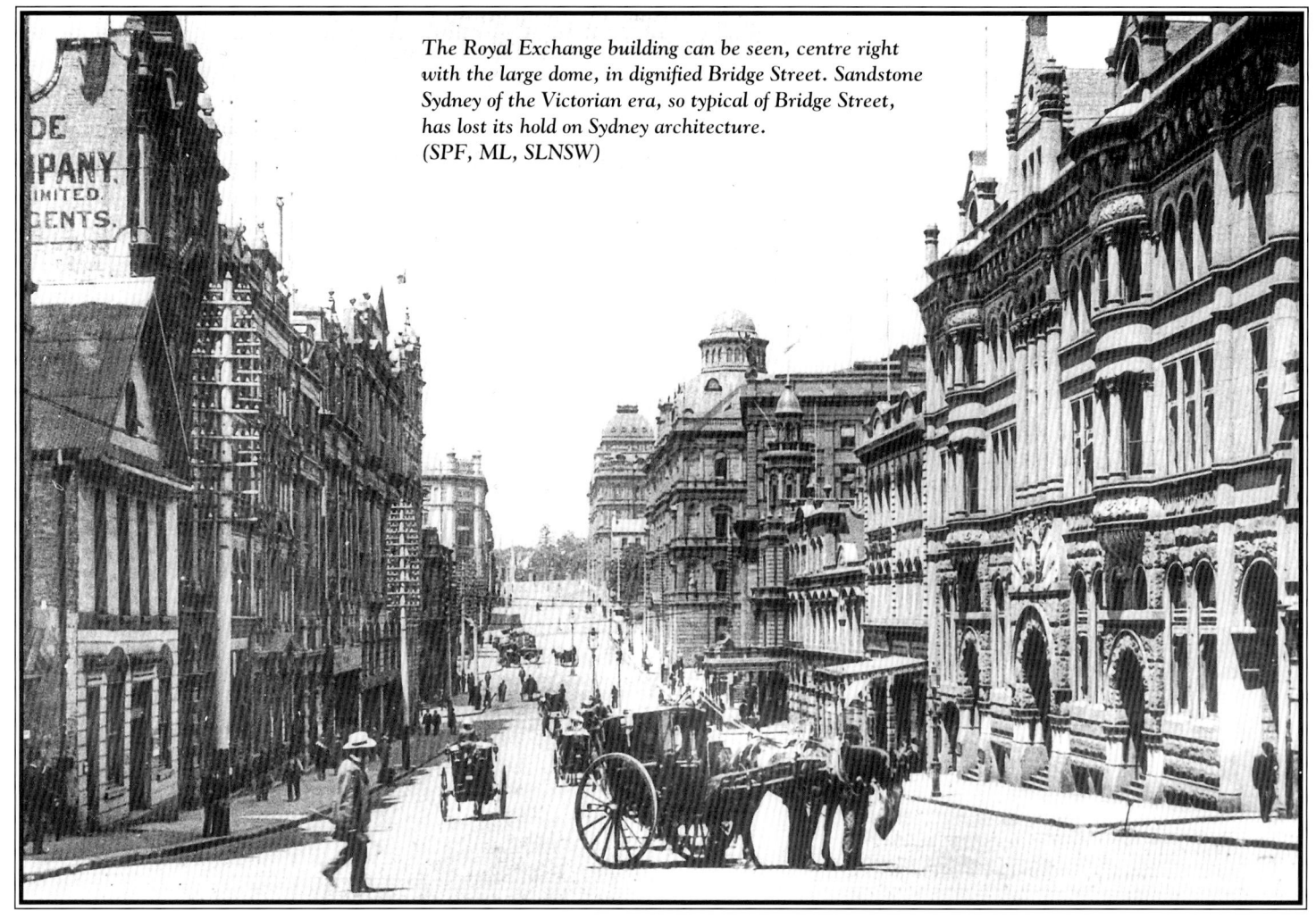

The Royal Exchange building can be seen, centre right with the large dome, in dignified Bridge Street. Sandstone Sydney of the Victorian era, so typical of Bridge Street, has lost its hold on Sydney architecture.
(SPF, ML, SLNSW)

In Touch with the First Fleet

HMS *Sirius* was the escorting flagship of the First Fleet. The gallant little vessel of 512 tons and 110 feet in length, sailed before the westerlies to Cape Town, via Cape Horn, to bring desperately needed provisions to the starving settlement.

On 7 March 1790, under the command of Captain Hunter, *Sirius* sailed for Norfolk Island to establish a penal settlement. She stood off the island in heavy seas for six days but managed to land her passengers and unload the stores before being driven onto a reef and smashed to pieces. Her crew struggled ashore in heavy surf and it was 11 months before they were brought back to Sydney.

The *Sirius'* anchor was recovered in 1907 and unveiled in Macquarie Place. A cannon close by was removed from the *Sirius* while she was in Sydney Cove. The anchor and the cannon are two surviving relics handled by seamen of the First Fleet.

This shady retreat off Bridge Street, where office workers now unwrap their lunchtime sandwiches, was chosen by Governor Macquarie as the colony's axis. He commissioned convict stonemason Edward Cureton to shape an obelisk from which all distances throughout the colony could be measured. It has stood since 1818. Commissioner Bigge considered it a waste of money and was critical of the neighbouring

In 1874 the house with the veranda in Macquarie Place on the right is part of the mansion belonging to wealthy emancipist Simeon Lord.

fountain, designed by Francis Greenway, where Mort's statue stands today. It would please the Commissioner to know it was ignominiously converted to a men's' urinal before being removed later in the century.

The association of Macquarie Place with the early traders seems to be the only justification for the stony presence of Thomas Sutcliffe Mort who has stared imperiously across Bridge Street since 1883. His name is of little significance to most Sydneysiders but he once held considerable influence in the affairs of the colony. Mort made his money from wool and was associated with a variety of enterprises including the first Sydney railway company. His two great achievements were the building of the first dry dock in Balmain in 1855 and his experiments in shipping refrigeration.

Australia's First Newspaper

'I gave permission to an ingenious man who manages the Government Printing press, to collect material in the form of a weekly newspaper.' Governor King's 'ingenious man' was George Howe who produced the colony's first newspaper, the *Sydney Gazette*, in 1803.

Howe was born in the West Indies and worked as a newspaper printer until he was transported for stealing from a mercer's shop. He arrived in Sydney in 1800; his wife and young son followed but she died on the voyage.

The printing press Governor Phillip brought with him remained idle for eight years until a man named George Hughes was found who could print government orders. Howe, who took over from Hughes, suggested publishing a weekly newspaper. Governor King approved on condition he censored its contents. The first edition, produced from a lean-to alongside Government House, appeared 5 March 1803. Howe was assisted by his eight year old son, Robert, who sorted type fonts perched on a high stool.

The four page, sixpenny paper contained government orders, shipping news, court reports and advertising. The first issue gave an account of the capture of 15 runaway Irish convicts from Castle Hill who went on a rampage of looting and assault. A party of Aborigines discovered their hideaway.

Howe did everything - from writing and producing the paper, to delivering copies to subscribers. Sydney's population was 7 000 and the print run exceeded 300. Following the 'Rum Rebellion' and the unseating of Governor Bligh the *Sydney Gazette* ceased publication for nine months claiming a paper shortage.

'Thus we hope to prosper' the masthead motto read; Howe himself prospered but not entirely through his newspaper. The paper moved into premises in Macquarie Place and Governor Macquarie paid him an annual wage of £60. The woman with whom he shared a de facto relationship died having borne him five children. A few years later he married a wealthy widow with five children of her own. Together the couple would have two more children. Apart from those who had grown up and married, the entire brood lived in a house at 96 George Street.

In 1813 Howe published the colony's first popular book: *Birds of New South Wales and Their Natural History* which contained 18 colour plates. Howe also published an anthology: *First Fruits of Australian Poetry*. He was planning the colony's first magazine when he died of dropsy in May 1821 leaving a comfortable estate of £4000.

His son Robert, who had grown into a dissolute young man until he found religion, carried on the paper and adopted a highly moral tone which drove some of his readers away. Robert seemed to invite legal action and on one occasion was whipped up George Street by Dr Redfern for derogatory remarks published in the *Gazette*. The doctor was fined 30 shillings.

In 1827 Robert wrote self-pityingly that he was debilitated through 'mental anxiety' and 'unexpected domestic disquietude' and appointed an editor to reduce his workload. Two years later while fishing off Pinchgut in Sydney Harbour, Robert Howe's boat capsized and he drowned. Curiously his youngest son, Alfred Australia Howe, was taken by a shark in the Harbour.

Robert's wife became proprietor of the *Gazette* when the circulation, having exceeded 600, was in decline. In 1836 the *Gazette* came into the possession of Richard Jones, a wealthy merchant, who used the paper to attack the liberal policies of Governor Bourke.

Several newspapers then appeared: the *Sydney (Morning) Herald* outselling them all. The last issue of the *Sydney Gazette* was published 20 October 1841 during the economic depression.

Australia's first newspaper has provided historians with an invaluable day-to-day record of the colony's early progress.

The Conservatorium of Music

In 1817 Governor Macquarie asked Francis Greenway to design stables, to accommodate 30 horses, for a proposed Government House. The Governor laid the foundation stone in December, four days after he assured Lord Bathurst he would not proceed with the construction of a new Government House. The stables, modelled as a castle-keep with high castellated walls and octagonal corner towers, was completed three years later.

Did Francis Greenway get carried away in his design or was it a deliberate ploy by the Governor to convince the Colonial Secretary it would be necessary to build a grand Government House. To a visiting Frenchman entering the Harbour it appeared to be a small fortress perched on a ridge. Commissioner Bigge, part of whose brief was to curb the Governor's spending, tut-tutted over the stables' 'useless magnificence'. Macquarie was secretly delighted.

When the new Government House was completed in 1845, the stables seemed less incongruous. They were in use until 1908 when architect, W.L. Vernon, redesigned the building as a Conservatorium of Music by covering-in the courtyard and turning it into a concert hall in 1914, under the musical direction of Belgian-born Henri Verbrugghen.

Rear view of the Government House stables which housed the Light Horse before the building was transformed into the Conservatorium of Music in 1914.

Watercolour by John Rae of the incomplete Government House in 1842.

Fit for a Governor

A succession of governors had complained about the inadequacies of aging Government House until the new residence was ready for occupation in June 1845. Enfolded in a dark wood, its broad lawns sloping to the Harbour foreshore, the Tudor Gothic 'castle' brought English medieval romanticism to the colony. Its critics saw it as a frowning military fortress; a recent writer thinks it looks like a haunted house.

Government House was designed in England by Edward Blore who never visited Sydney. Construction was supervised by the Colonial Architect, Mortimer Lewis. Gothic arches support the slate roof and a stone-paved, cloistered veranda runs along its northern perimeter. Today Government House, with high sandstone walls crowned by battlements, is a permanent reminder of our British past.

The handsome interior, finished in Australian cedar and local marble, has portraits of every governor who has occupied the house, beginning with Governor George Gipps. According to the records not one of them complained about their regal abode.

When the NSW Labor Government came to power in the 1990s one of its first actions was to open the vice-regal residence to the public: the current Governor is domiciled in his private home. The decision brought a flurry of protests at the time. Today Government House is managed by the NSW Historic Houses Trust.

Government House seen from the west side of Circular Quay in 1870.
(SPF, ML, SLNSW)

Sydney's Garden Retreat

The First Fleeters couldn't imagine a future Sydney, but Governor Arthur Phillip had the foresight to provide a 'green belt', reaching along the eastern perimeter of the settlement from the Harbour to present Oxford Street. Governor Phillip's 'open space' became the Botanic Gardens, the Domain and Hyde Park for which generations of Sydneysiders are eternally grateful. The Royal Botanic Gardens (the 'Royal' added in 1959) has a quiet history. A single turbulence occurred in 1835 when Colonial Botanist, Richard Cunningham, was clubbed to death by Aborigines when he strayed from one of Surveyor-General Mitchell's exploratory expeditions. Bickering, bureaucratic bungling and all manner of modern encroachments have dogged the history of the Botanic Gardens until as recently as 1980 when the Domain Trust Act settled once and for all the authority and rights of the Gardens.

There was urgency in Governor Phillip's order to clear nine acres around the inlet east of Sydney Cove. It was to be the government granary providing sorely needed wheat and barley but the soil was poor and rust ultimately damaged the wheat. Fortunately the rich earth at Rose Hill, (Parramatta) proved more receptive.

The land at Farm Cove remained government property and by the time Governor William Bligh and his daughter Mary, a keen gardener, occupied Government House, the area was laid out with trees and shrubbery edged by shady walkways. In June 1816 Governor Macquarie declared the road to Mrs Macquarie's Chair open and the Botanic Gardens date from that time. To ensure future governors maintained their privacy Macquarie built a stone wall enclosing the Government House garden and former government farm. A section of Macquarie's wall survives as have some swamp mahogany trees beneath which Mrs Macquarie's carriage conveyed her to her celebrated lookout 'chair'.

The dining room in Government House taken in 1870. When Government House opened on 26 June 1845 visitors marvelled at the splendour of Edward Blore's architecture and the furnishings.

In 1817 Governor Macquarie appointed Charles Fraser, a private with the 46th Regiment, Superintendent of the Botanic Gardens. Fraser approached the job enthusiastically, travelling about the country, sometimes joining exploratory expeditions, collecting specimens. In four years the Gardens were clearly defined within Government House grounds, entry restricted to 'the respectable class of inhabitants'.

The Gardens were enlarged and opened to the public in 1831, the year Charles Fraser died. Richard Cunningham arrived from England to take up the post of Colonial Botanist. When he was killed his brother, Allan, a botanical collector for the Royal Gardens at Kew who spent some years collecting in NSW, arrived to take up the job but resigned in disgust when senior government officials insisted large sections be used for cultivating their vegetables.

Directors came and went until the arrival from England of 27-year-old Charles Moore in 1848. His presence was scarcely welcome. John Bidwell, 'a gentleman of superior qualifications', had been appointed Director of the Botanic Gardens when a dispatch arrived from Earl Grey in London informing Governor Gipps of Moore's appointment. The locals were angered by this outside interference but Bidwell, who had held the position for six months, was posted off to Queensland where he later died from exposure after being lost in the bush.

Fortunately Moore's dedication and considerable tact won over the authorities. The Governor was so pleased with the young man's achievements in the first year, he wrote: 'I considered the zeal and efficiency he has displayed in getting the gardens in order deserving of the commendation of the Government.'

The new Director had a sea wall constructed around Farm Cove reclaiming the tidal flat that reached to the present kiosk. Tons of silt from Sydney Cove and filling from demolished buildings was used over decades before completion in 1878.

In the early 1850s Moore lost most of his workmen; even the promise of extra wages failed to stop them downing tools and rushing off to the gold fields.

When life returned to normal a small zoo was introduced. Located in the present Succulent Garden it included a variety of birds, a monkey house and a Chinese deer. It was the genesis of Taronga Park Zoo and in 1883 it moved to the new Zoological Gardens in Moore Park and then, in November 1916, transferred across the Harbour to Taronga Park. One inmate of the original zoo was an ancient tortoise that was left behind to wander at will through the shrubbery until it died in 1967.

Another of Charles Moore's trials was the burning of the Garden Palace in September 1882 when 30 000 ornamental plants established around the building were destroyed.

In December 1885, following complaints of hooliganism, strict regulations warned 'No person in a state of intoxication, or of reputed bad character, or who is not cleanly and decently dressed' should enter the Gardens. Neither would anyone be admitted who 'shall behave in an improper or offensive manner, or use bad language, or commit any act of indecency therein'.

In the 48 years he was Director, Charles Moore elevated the status of the Botanic Gardens largely because of his dedication to the job and his engaging charm. He retired in 1896 and died at his home in Queen Street, Woollahra nine years later age 84, having left his mark on the Botanic Gardens for future generations.

Moore's position was taken by another competent administrator, Joseph Henry Maiden, who reigned over the Gardens for 28 years in which time he travelled to Europe to obtain specimens from valuable early Australian collections including those gathered at Botany Bay by Joseph Banks in 1770. He opened the new Herbarium Building in 1901.

The Botanic Gardens made little headway during the Depression years and World War II. In the postwar building boom, director Robert Anderson, appointed in 1945, improved conditions and fought off government incursions.

In 1988 the Rose Garden, with close to 200 varieties, opened on the site of the old Palace Garden.

In 1978 the administration of the Gardens was transferred from the Department of Agriculture to the Premier's Department. Two years later the passing of the Royal Botanic Gardens and Domain Trust Act ensured the sovereignty of the Gardens for all time.

Mothers and daughters rest on the lawns of the Botanic Gardens facing Farm Cove, at the turn of the century. (National Library of Australia)

MACQUARIE STREET 45

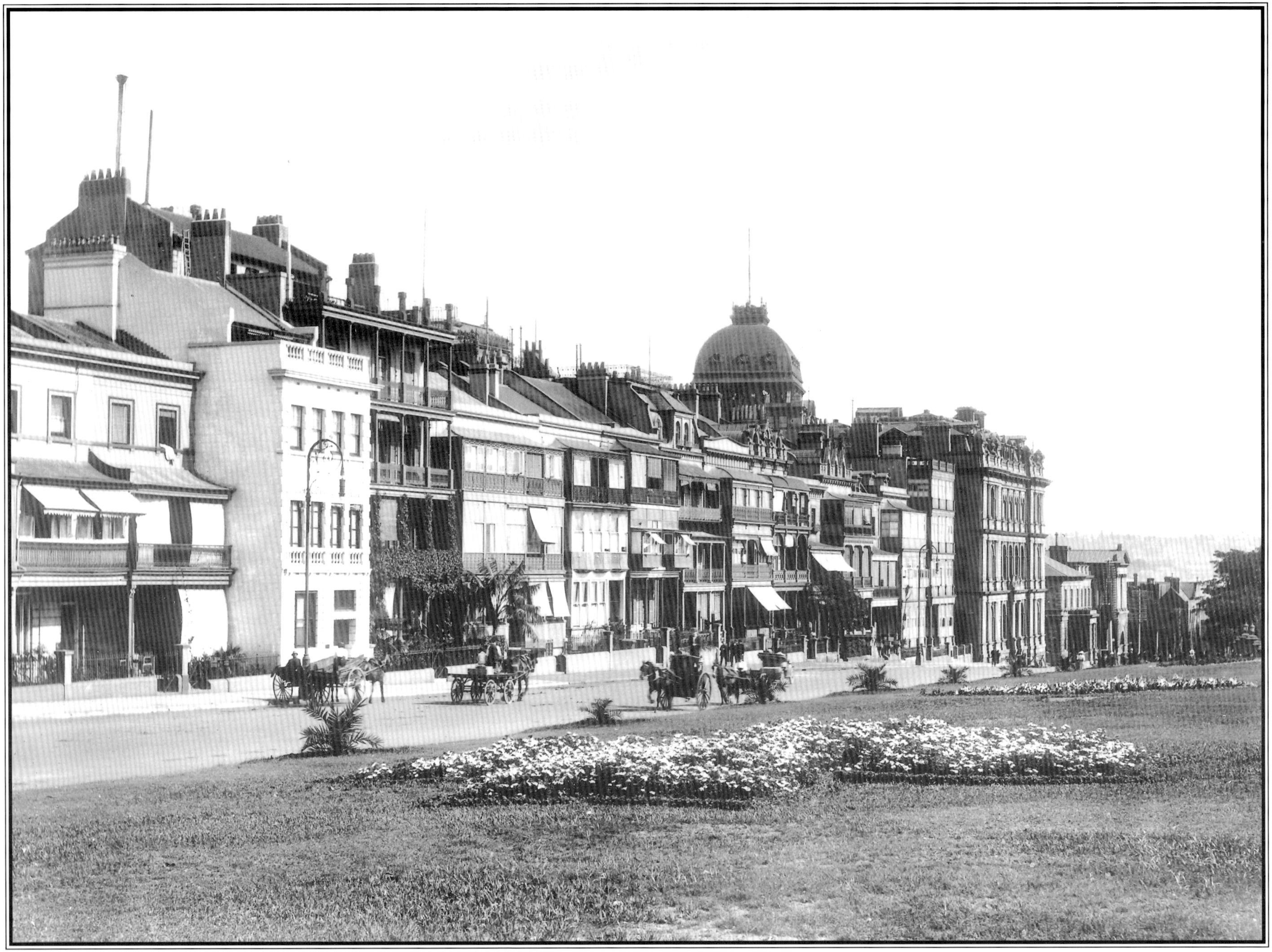

'The Palace is Burning!'

Once upon a time a splendid palace reigned in Sydney's Botanic Gardens. It occupied five acres and stretched from the Conservatorium of Music to the foot of the present Mitchell Library. The Garden Palace was built to house the Sydney International Exhibition inviting the world to inspect the colony's rich primary output and witness its advances in industry and science.

The *Sydney Morning Herald* considered it 'flattering to our self-esteem' that so many nations responded to the government's invitation; even the other Australian colonies lent their support although Melbourne hastily followed with its own exhibition.

The design of the building by James Barnet was based on London's Crystal Palace built in 1854 (destroyed by fire in 1936). It featured four giant towers around a high central roof dome looming behind pine and fig trees. Not everyone was pleased with Sydney's new palace; many resented the fact the gargantuan structure not only encroached on the Gardens, it blotted out some of the city's loveliest Harbour views.

The Garden Palace was intended to be a temporary building when the Governor, Lord Loftus, opened it on 17 September 1879 but when the last of the exhibition's one million visitors walked out on closing day, 20 April 1880, it had become a permanent fixture in everyone's minds. Sir Henry Parkes said the government intended to use if for 'the recreation of the people'. The auditorium was used for concerts, balls and public meetings; and government departmental records were stored in the basement.

At 3 am on the 22 September 1882 two constables making their rounds along Macquarie Street called into the Garden Palace to say goodnight to the watchman Mr Kirchen. All was quiet when they left soon after. At 5.30 am Mr Kirchen locked the door of the building and walked to the gate where he met the day watchman who came to relieve him. The two men stopped for a chat when one noticed smoke billowing around the grey roof dome. They ran to the building and unlocked the door:

'I cannot describe it,' said one of the watchmen. 'There was a great cloud of smoke and an enormous burst of fire.' Flames from the basement shot up through the fountain aperture. Fire brigades from various parts of the city galloped to the scene but the firemen could only 'stand still and gaze' at the raging inferno. The heat was so intense that windows snapped in houses along Macquarie Street. Ashes and charred wood were blown for miles around. In less than four hours the Garden Palace was a smouldering ruin and Macquarie Street residents got back their harbour views.

Some thought the fire was in protest against the building and its location; for years it was rumoured the fire was started by someone anxious to destroy the convict records stored in the basement. Valuable scientific records, the work of Reverend William Branwhite Clarke, were lost together with 300 paintings.

In a few short years it was as if the Garden Palace had never existed until a commemorative garden was created on the site. The central fountain, a water pipe and the reconstructed gates are all that remain of Sydney's palace.

Left: Two dozen three-storey gentlemen's residences were built in the 1850s of which History House, 133 Macquarie Street is the last remaining. First occupied by Dr William Bland, various medical practitioners lived there until it was acquired by the Royal Australian Historical Society in 1970. (Macleay Museum)
Right: Interior of the Garden Palace. (GPO, ML, SLNSW)

Palace Splendid. Sydney's Garden Palace built for the 1879-80 International Exhibition, the first of its kind in the southern hemisphere, was situated between the Conservatorium of Music and the State Library of NSW.

Lost glory: The remains of the Garden Palace after the fire on 22 September 1882. Macquarie Street residents got back their Harbour views.

Mitchell's Library

Mitchell had a full black beard and wore dark clothes usually topped by a black bowler hat, according to Sydney bookseller, the late Jim Tyrrell. He actually looked like a book collector; perhaps it was the way he peered at things. One rarely saw him unless it was in a bookshop because Mitchell was something of a recluse and booksellers usually brought their latest acquisitions up to his house in Darlinghurst Road.

Posterity has benefited from Mitchell's grand passion; his magnificent collection of Australiana brought the Mitchell Library into existence and today it is recognised as one of the world's greatest collections of books and documents relating to a single region.

David Scott Mitchell was born in the officer's quarters of the Sydney Hospital in 1836. His father was a Scottish army surgeon from whom David inherited his great love of books. At the age of 16, he was among the first 24 students to enter Sydney University. Called to the bar in 1858 his shy, retiring personality deterred him from going into practice. Years later he is said to have turned down the position of Attorney-General.

Never a strong boy he enjoyed taking part in sport, especially cricket, but his real love was literature, particularly relating to the Elizabethan period. He also wrote occasional verse. He met and fell in love with Emily Manning, a judge's daughter who wrote under the name of 'Australie'. Enchanted by her 'clarion words' and delighted to discover a kindred spirit, the shy bachelor invited her to 'mingle in the crush of life'. She refused his eloquent offer of marriage and the shattered suitor buried himself deeper in his books.

He was in his early thirties when his father died leaving him the family property in Cumberland Street at the Rocks. He already received a substantial private income from the sale of his father's extensive property in the Hunter Valley. David moved into 17 Darlinghurst Road where he pursued his hobby relentlessly; demanding booksellers gave him first choice of their latest arrivals and went to any length and cost in pursuit of a particular title.

He not only collected books, he read them all and the story goes that Sarah, his housekeeper, interrupted his reading to inform him the balcony had collapsed into the street. Without glancing up David told her to call a carter and get him to remove the rubble.

Mitchell netted Australiana from around the world, not only books but diaries, letters, pamphlets, charts and coins. In November 1898 his collection had grown to 61,000 items. He told the Public Library Trustees he would bequeath his entire collection on condition the government erected an appropriate building to house it. As anticipated, the government procrastinated and Mitchell amended his bequest stating the library building should be completed within one year after his death. Mitchell's health was failing and the trustees persuaded the government to find a suitable site. The one chosen facing the Domain was near the Macquarie Street hospital where he was born. The foundation stone for the library was laid by the NSW Premier, Joseph Carruthers,

Books, books, books! There was barely room to move in David Mitchell's Darlinghurst houses's bedroom. (GPO, ML, SLNSW)

in 1906. Too ill to attend the ceremony; he endowed an additional £70 000 for the purchase of more books and documents. By the time the Mitchell Library opened on the 8 March 1910, David Scott Mitchell was dead but he lived long enough to see the building taking shape that would bear his name.

The story goes that in Mitchell's last moments Fred Wymark of Angus and Robertson appeared at his bedside clutching a copy of a title he had sought for years. A voice croaked, 'How much do you want for it Fred?' The price was £100 and Mitchell nodded. 'I must have it.' He died that night still clutching the slim volume of Barron Fields' *First Fruits of Australian Poetry*.

Returned soldiers march past the nine-year-old Mitchell Library building in 1919. It was built to house David Mitchell's vast collection of Australiana.

The Rum Hospital

Within weeks of the landing of the First Fleet a makeshift hospital was erected on the western arm of Sydney Cove. When the Second Fleet disgorged its cargo of half-starved convicts from the overcrowded, stifling holds, many expired as they breathed the fresh air and almost 500 dead and dying were carried over to the hospital lawns. A portable hospital, transported in the accompanying supply ship, was of little help and a hundred tents were hastily pitched to cope with the sufferers of 'scurvy, fevers, violent purging and flux'.

The Second Fleet also brought the first detachment of the NSW Corps, a regiment specially raised for service in the colony. Lieutenant John Macarthur, 22, who would exert a powerful influence over the infant colony, accompanied the regiment along with his bride. Governor Hunter had the hospital rebuilt on a stone foundation to serve government employees and the convict community.

When Major-General Lachlan Macquarie, the new Governor, landed in December 1809, the hospital was in a state of the 'most ruinous decay'. One of his first aims was to build hospital 'of noble proportions' in keeping with the growing population. He chose a seven acre site in a street he named after himself. The design featured three main blocks, each of two storeys, with shady verandas. The central building was to contain the hospital, and those either side were to provide quarters for surgeons and staff; the whole was surrounded by a nine foot wall.

Officers of the NSW Corps had held much of the colony's affairs in their hands. When a cargo of spirits arrived, they bought quantities, according to rank, at the government cost price of three shillings a gallon retailing at 40 shillings a gallon: a profit of 1 200 per cent!. When Macquarie arrived with his 73rd Highland Regiment the ignominious 'Rum Corps' embarked for England and the new governor attempted to control the spirit trade by licensing vendors and imposing import duty.

In July 1810 former government employees Alexander Riley, Garnham Blaxcell and D'Arcy Wentworth submitted an unusual tender. They were prepared to build the hospital, without cost, in return for monopoly of the rum trade. They asked for permission to import 45 000 gallons over a period of three years and the government to provide them with 20 convict labourers.

Having broken one monopoly in spirituous liquors the Governor would be encouraging another. Was the welfare of the sick and needy to be paid for at the price of drunkenness? Macquarie, determined to have his hospital at all costs, accepted their offer. No figures exist to prove inebriation increased.

Macquarie laid the foundation for the main hospital building in October 1811. As it neared completion the *Sydney Gazette* considered it 'so well proportioned as to gratify the eye of taste and the mind of science'. Francis Greenway, the convict architect, attracted the Governor's attention and eventual patronage by a blistering criticism of the building that later proved to be full of defects.

It was five years before patients were brought up from Dawes Point to the four wards in the new

Macquarie Street with the Rum Hospital on the left. It became Parliament House and the Mint. Hyde Park Barracks (on the right) was built separately in 1817.

hospital each with beds for 20 patients although it wasn't long before twice the number were squeezed in.

Dysentery was the main complaint in those days. There were also many sufferers from rheumatism and venereal disease. One of the less tasteful duties of the medical staff was for a member to be present at a flogging in the courtyard of neighbouring Hyde Park Barracks. The first four lashes always drew blood.

Dr William Redfern, a naval surgeon transported for a minor role in the Mutiny of the Nore, was put in charge and D'Arcy Wentworth, a free settler with limited medical qualifications, made infrequent visits as the colony's Principal Surgeon.

Conditions in the hospital quickly deteriorated. Cooking was conducted in the wards, poorly washed bed linen was changed once a week, dressings were frequently thrown under the bed. With no indoor lavatories those who were too weak to walk had to crawl outside. Patients were subjected to screams of amputees in those days before anaesthetics. There was no segregation of the sexes and patients were locked in the wards from sunset until dawn. Sexual activity was rife in the wards, and rape commonplace. The 'depraved and drunken' convict wardsmen and nurses frequently stole from the patients.

The arrival of Dr James Bowman, following the resignation of Redfern and Wentworth turned this 'Hades' back into a hospital.

Bowman, a naval surgeon with sound qualifications was an able administrator who proceeded to make order out of chaos. In 1836 the hospital was placed under control of the military for the next 12 years. Transportation had ceased and remaining convict patients were moved to Parramatta. The hospital became the Sydney Infirmary for impoverished free men and women.

The colony was in desperate need of nurses and the Colonial Secretary, Henry Parkes, appealed to Florence Nightingale to assist in recruiting trained nurses. Remembering Australia's generous contribution to the Crimea fund, Miss Nightingale sent Lucy Osburn, 32, as Lady Supervisor in charge of five nursing sisters. The group arrived in March 1868 and within a week were attending the Duke of Edinburgh, wounded by an assassin's bullet at Clontarf.

Lucy Osburn was dismayed at the verminous state of the hospital now sorely in need of repair. Unpleasant odours rose from the sewers and kitchens were thick with grease. In nine months the indomitable Miss Osburn had trained 16 local nurses in the Nightingale method.

Although Parkes was charmed by her 'bright, ingenuous manner' she found less sympathy among the male-dominated hospital hierarchy who put every obstacle in her way. In 1873 a Royal Commission accused the management committee of 'utter neglect' and condemned the conditions including the 'horrible operating room'. Lucy Osburn was completely vindicated.

The central section of Macquarie's hospital was demolished in 1879 and the foundation stone was laid by the Governor, Lord Loftus, who announced it would be known as the Sydney Hospital which was declared open 10 August 1894. By that time other fine hospitals were built in Sydney including the Royal Prince Alfred which opened in Camperdown in 1882.

A lone watchman contemplates Macquarie Street from the balcony of Parliament House in 1871. With Sydney's modest population of 53 000, the streets were seldom crowded. (National Library of Australia)

Greenway's Masterpiece

The Hyde Park Barracks is Sydney's major surviving link with its convict past. For 30 years men 'dressed alike in a garb of hodden grey or duck' embroidered with initials HPB, shuffled through its stone gateway to toil from dawn till dusk hewing rock, mending roads and making bricks.

The barracks was the work of a short, auburn-haired convict architect whose ingenuity and talent won him recognition and prestige but whose petulant personality and uncompromising arrogance led to his ultimate downfall.

Greenway's ancestors were West Country stonemasons and builders. Francis had conducted an architectural consultancy in Bristol until he was declared bankrupt. In desperation, he forged a contract for which he was arrested and sentenced to death in 1812. He arrived in Sydney two years later, his sentence commuted to transportation for 14 years. His wife and three children followed.

The young architect came to the notice of Governor Macquarie who gave him a ticket-of-leave enabling Greenway to set up practice in George Street. Greenway's strident criticism of existing public works invoked considerable hostility but the Governor appointed him Civil Architect in 1816. The position provided an income of 21 shillings a week, a house below The Rocks and a horse.

Greenway's first project was the Macquarie Lighthouse (demolished in 1883) at South Head which he used as a training workshop for the colony's desperately needed masons.

Macquarie saw in Greenway an opportunity to fulfil his ambition to transform the 'decayed and dilapidated' settlement into a civilised, self-reliant colony Britain could be proud of. This called for a new Government House, to settle Macquarie's complaint that 'no private gentleman in the colony is so ill-accommodated as I'. Greenway designed a castle overlooking the Harbour but it only got as far as the castellated Gothic stables (now the Conservatorium of Music) before the Colonial Office ordered the Governor to cut down spending.

Greenway and the Governor had their heads together on other projects such as a spacious barracks for male convicts. The Hyde Park Barracks took two years to build and opened on King George IV's birthday, 4 June 1819. Finished in soft red sandstone brick, the barracks' bold, uncomplicated Georgian lines were eminently suited to its backdrop of blue sky and bright sunlight, adding a touch of grandeur to the haphazard township.

The main dormitory block and guardrooms stood in a courtyard surrounded by a ten foot stone wall. The three-storey building accommodated 600; in time a further 400 were pressed in. The flogging post was brought up from the Lumber Yard - on the southern corner of George and Bridge Streets - but 'the convicts found means, either by threats or by bribes to the flogger, to diminish their severity'.

Soon after the convicts were housed in their new establishment, the number of town robberies dropped dramatically. The Governor was so pleased that he allowed Greenway's wife, Mary, to persuade him to grant her husband a full pardon.

Robbery was rife among the inmates; stolen items were often tossed over the wall to associates. According to the cynical Commissioner Bigge: 'The association of so many depraved and desperate characters in one place is an evil that is complained of even by the convicts themselves.'

With the end of the transportation system in 1840 the barracks fell into neglect and it became an intrusion in the centre of the growing township. In January 1848 the remaining convicts were removed to Cockatoo Island and for years the barracks was a staging centre for thousands of single female immigrants from Britain.

In the late 'eighties the interior was partitioned to provide courtroom facilities and Government legal departments spilled into a collection of unsightly temporary buildings. The question of demolition of Greenway's masterpiece was regularly raised, the last time in 1946.

Thirty years later the legal appendages were swept away and work began on the long overdue restoration of the old barracks. Today the building remains a tribute to Greenway's artistry and imagination and is one of Sydney's tourist attractions. An open-air restaurant occupies the courtyard which once echoed to the swish of the flogger's cat-o'-nine-tails. The building is now in the care of the Historic Houses Trust.

The Spire of St James'

On one hand the animated, grey-haired military officer who had elevated the ramshackle settlement into a cohesive colony; on the other, the aloof, austere Commissioner, whose orders were to bring a stern constraint to the Governor's humanitarian regime. Differences were put aside for the laying of the foundation stone for St James' Church, 7 October 1819.

Five weeks earlier Governor Macquarie laid the foundation stone for St Andrew's Cathedral but Commissioner John Bigge, told to curb Macquarie's spending, proposed the courthouse, designed by Francis Greenway, should become a church instead. To give the structure an ecclesiastical air, the disgruntled Greenway added a tower and a spire that dominated Sydney's skyline for decades. The architect was upset when his name was left off the building when that of Lachlan Macquarie was inevitably included.

Close proximity of the church to officialdom saw a congregation of mainly administrators and military officers. Convicts, restricted to their own gallery, entered through an underground passage from Hyde Park Barracks. In 1832 distinguished architect John Verge added a vestry in harmony with Greenway's design

The Governor's Sunday presence drew important citizens, many of whom rented a family pew. One was Edward Smith Hall, the outspoken publisher of the *Sydney Monitor*, whose strident criticism of the administration earned the enmity of Governor Darling.

St James' in 1856 still held its prestigious reputation. Influential families arranged christenings and marriages there. At night people crossing Hyde Park left the church in groups as muggings and robberies were rife in the park in the 1850s. Photographed here by Henry King, looking down King Street.

Another of Hall's 'victims' was Archdeacon Thomas Hobbes Scott whose dubious acquisition of vast land grants and support of the autocratic Darling made him a prime target for Hall's pen.

On a Sunday evening in July 1828, Hall arrived to find the family pew locked and a beadle standing guard. He vaulted over and forced the lock, enabling his three daughters to enter. The following Sunday three beadles stood armed with staves. The Hall family defiantly followed the sermon seated on the altar steps. The next Sunday Hall forced the lock but Archdeacon Hobbes was to have the last word. He had the pew boarded up.

The Reverend Robert Allwood arrived in 1840 to serve St James' for 44 years, the longest serving incumbent. By the time Allwood departed, a city had grown up around the church.

In the mid-1890s Varney Parkes, architect son of Sir Henry, rebuilt the spire, weathering the copper sheeting to match the original. In 1901 the entire interior of the church was rebuilt and the pews, the rent for which contributed to church coffers, were finally removed.

The opening of St James' Station in 1926 and the proximity of David Jones Elizabeth Street Store increased activity in that part of the city. Another sign of the times was the appointment of the first Australian-born rector, the Reverend E.J. Davidson, who was widely known through his radio broadcasts in the war years.

In the 1950s amends were made to the creator, when Francis Greenway's name was inscribed on a wall tablet.

Lingering Legalities

'A new, large, elegant and commodious Brick Built Court house, two storeys high with all the requisite apartments and offices attached ... will soon be completed,' reported Governor Macquarie. The courthouse, originally conceived as a parish school by Francis Greenway, was completed six years after the Governor departed in 1822.

Administration of justice was entrusted to the Judge Advocate and a jury of six officers; naval or military, similar to a court martial. In 1824 the first Lord Chief Justice, Francis Forbes, arrived with his family, carrying the Charter of Justice for NSW. The tall, cultured Forbes was the model judge; Judge Roger Therry praised him for his 'imperturbable calmness of temper, acute discrimination, and a thorough acquaintance with legal principles'.

Chief Justice Forbes came into conflict with Governor Darling over the Governor's attempt to restrict freedom of the press. Darling wanted to impose fourpence stamp duty on all newspapers in an attempt to curtail his arch enemies, the *Australian* and the *Monitor*, both highly critical of his administration. The Colonial Office in London supported Forbes but his health was impaired by the controversy and an excessive workload. He sailed for England where he appeared as a witness before the Parliamentary Committee on Transportation.

His health failed to improve and he returned to Sydney, having accepted a knighthood, where he died in 1841. The town of Forbes is named in his honour.

The Supreme Court building with multiple extensions was in a sorry state, time having eroded the mortar made from oyster shells. When Darlinghurst Courthouse opened in 1842 the old courthouse lost its significance but it failed to collapse and a brick and stucco colonnade was added.

The courthouse continued to house legal luminaries, in a Dickensian atmosphere, for more than 150 years, in spite of draughty corridors and leaky roofs, and refused to be intimidated when its 22-storey direct descendant opened across the road.

In the late 1970s the State Government spent $1.2 million restoring the building and converting the top of King Street into a pedestrian mall. The Greenway touch lingers in the unpretentious building's recessed wall panels and arches, its cedar joinery and geometric staircase. Even the petulant Mr Greenway couldn't object to that.

Morning peak hour traffic passes Greenway's courthouse on the corner of Elizabeth Street in 1882.
(Illustrated Sydney News)

The Georgian School

The Elizabeth Street block between Market and King Street was once owned by one-time housebreaker Thomas Rose. When the Shropshire-born baker's assistant was transported for life it proved a blessing for it gave him the opportunity to exercise his initiative. Ten years after his arrival he opened the Rose and Crown Inn on the present site of David Jones Store and was so successful he finished up owning the block.

When Commissioner Bigge told Governor Macquarie the planned charity school adjacent to St James' Church would be more appropriate as a courthouse, the Governor decided he would still have his school. He offered Thomas Rose 300 acres near Campbelltown in exchange for part of his Elizabeth Street site, a proposal the former convict grudgingly accepted.

Francis Greenway designed the large, two-storey Georgian schoolhouse surrounding it with a high wall. Named St James' Church of England School, it accommodated 400 male and 200 female students. The court commandeered several rooms while the courthouse was being built across the road. Privates Sudds and Thompson were found guilty of theft and Governor Darling ordered the two soldiers to work on the road gangs with iron collars attached by chains causing the death of Sudds and a public outcry.

From 1829 the building housed the Sydney Boys' Grammar School until they moved into their own building in College Street in 1857.

The Public Instruction Act of 1880 provided for the establishment of high schools for boys and girls. In October 1883 Sydney Boys' High and Sydney Girls' High occupied Greenway's schoolhouse. Ten years later the boys moved to a building in Mary Anne Street, Ultimo but the headmistress of the girls' school, Miss Wheatley Walker, refused to move her girls to what she considered a rough locality with its larrikin gangs. The girls remained in Elizabeth Street until 1921 when their new home at Moore Park was completed.

This building, the future site of David Jones in Elizabeth Street, was built in Governor Macquarie's time, occupied by the Supreme Court, the Presbyterian Church and used as a Catholic schoolroom. In 1883 Sydney Girls High opened here and remained until 1920 when this famous school moved to Moore Park, the site of Sydney's old zoo. (National Library of Australia)

AROUND HYDE PARK 59

Hyde Park was a popular venue for lovers and larrikins in the 1870s.
(National Library of Australia)

Tranquillity reigns over Hyde Park's 40 acres in 1871, roaring traffic and rearing office blocks still half a century away. The park's walkways at the southern end are already defined, soon there will be trees and blossoming flowerbeds. That's the Australian museum on the left. (SPF, ML, SLNSW)

AROUND HYDE PARK   61

Residential dwellings line Elizabeth Street. Until the 1880s and the advancements in public transport most people lived in the central city area. (SPF, ML, SLNSW)

The Bushman's Bible

The two young men were ideally suited for their business venture. Geelong-born J.F. Archibald was intense, intelligent, industrious, and his partner, John Haynes, was enterprising, outgoing and argumentative. They were employed on the editorial staff of the *Evening News* when they decided to produce a publication different from all the rest. They raised £40 as deposit on a second-hand press, bought some used typefaces and rented the old Scandinavian Hall. Archibald handled the editorial, working on a packing case; Haynes pushed advertising and circulation.

There was nothing sensational about the first issue of the *Bulletin*, priced at fourpence for eight sparsely illustrated pages, except for its impish comments which appealed to a public used to conservative, serious-minded journals. It contained a lengthy account of the hanging of the bushranger Captain Moonlight in Darlinghurst Gaol. The print run of 4000 sold out. Before long the partners were plagued by lawsuits and financial problems.

The leaders were written by the prestigious pen of W.H. Traill, Reuter's Sydney agent. It was he who saved the *Bulletin* from bankruptcy when he took over as proprietor employing both Archibald and Haynes. Traill's five year editorship led to the *Bulletin*'s spectacular success. He acquired the services of celebrated black-and-white artist Livingstone Hopkins, 'Hop', from the USA and Phil May from England, who were later joined by Australia's Norman Lindsay.

The *Bulletin* went against many of the establishment's pet causes. It was republican in outlook and supported Home Rule for Ireland. Later it bitterly opposed Australia's involvement in the Boer War. The paper which had begun as something of a lark, saw its responsibility on national issues but was quick to see the humorous side of an argument.

J.F. Archibald and Henry Lawson in 1915.

John Haynes resigned, following differences with Traill, and entered politics. In 1883, during one of his frequent bouts of ill-health, Archibald made a trip to London where he met, and later married, Rosa Frankenstein. It was an ill-matched affair which eventually brought Rosa to alcoholism. When Traill left the *Bulletin* to follow Haynes into the political arena in 1886, Archibald ran the paper in partnership with William McLeod.

The *Bulletin* boycotted the centenary celebrations of 1888, it also attacked 'unchristian' Christianity, with comic parsons tripping through its cartoons, and the 'capitalist' was illustrated as a bloated, top-hatted bigot. The paper itself was not free of bigotry. It was bitterly anti-Chinese and anti-coloured, except for Aborigines, and some of its cartoons had a distinct anti-semitic flavour.

The *Bulletin* was welcome reading in the bush, earning the title of 'The Bushman's Bible'. When Australia's population reached its first million, the *Bulletin*'s circulation reached 80 000. The *Bulletin* came into its own in the 1890s. Appreciation of home-grown talent was part of the new spirit of nationalism, writers jostling to appear in its columns. Some became famous: 'Banjo' Paterson, Henry Lawson, A.G. Stevens and cartoonist David Low. In 1903 Archibald handed over editorship to James Edmond and concentrated on his monthly literary off-shoot, *Lone Hand* which appeared in 1907. It was Edmond who changed the masthead motto from 'Australia for the Australians' to 'Australia for the White Man'.

A new generation of writers were emerging:

Work in progress on the City Circle underground railway which opened in 1926. The Archibald Fountain came later. Archibald died in 1919 leaving £90 000 to create the Archibald Prize and to build the Archibald Fountain. (NSW Government Printer)

C J Dennis, Dorothea Mackellar, Hugh McCrae and Mary Gilmore all appeared in the *Bulletin*. Meantime Archibald suffered a mental breakdown and spent months in Callan Park Asylum. He was discharged in 1910 and his wife died the following year.

In 1919 the irreverent *Smith's Weekly* began reporting the activities of a postwar, suburban Australia. It was even more outspoken than the *Bulletin*. Archibald died later that year leaving £90 000 in his will to present Australia with an annual prize for portrait painting and an elaborate fountain in Hyde Park.

Samuel Prior edited the *Bulletin* from 1933. Prior was a financial journalist with a love of literature. He introduced the *Bulletin* prize for novelists. He had acquired Archibald's share of the *Bulletin* and from 1927 the Prior family held financial control. In 1960 Sir Frank Packer made the proprietors 'an offer they couldn't refuse'. The circulation was below 30 000 and the paper was living on its past reputation. The paper was dramatically reconstructed, the first gesture by new editor, Donald Horne, was to remove 'Australia for the White Man' from the masthead.

The *Bulletin* became a news magazine, tuned to Australia's growing international influence and recognising its place in south-east asian affairs. The old *Bulletin* may have died but no publication contributed so much to the shaping of Australia's national character as 'The Bushman's Bible'.

1106 St Mary's Cathedral Sydney (H. King)

Above: Commuters spill from the newly opened St James underground railway station in 1926 and head for the shops and offices. Some things never change. (News Limited)

Right: 'Far down below the roots of the tallest fig tree in Hyde Park a strange new breathing world glittered with light this morning, with one great roar the underground railway woke to life.' Sydney Sun 20 December 1926.

Facing Page: Sydney's Catholic community was delighted when Governor Macquarie laid the foundation stone for St Mary's Cathedral in 1821. The building was destroyed by fire in June 1865 and fire again gutted a temporary structure four years later. Building of the present St Mary's began in December 1868. In 1999 the completion of the spires began in preparation for the 21st century. (National Library of Australia)

'Curious and Rare'

Considering that the continent was rich in mineral deposits and geological curiosities, successive governors were slow in supporting research: it was left to interested gentlemen of means.

The arrival of Colonial Secretary, Alexander Macleay, with his unique insect collection, aroused interest in local natural history and his Elizabeth Bay House became a centre for discussion and a base for visiting scientists.

A shed adjacent to Judge Advocate Forbes' old house in Bridge Street, facing Macquarie Place, housed the first local specimens and William Holmes, a zoologist whose career ended when he accidentally shot himself while collecting specimens at Moreton Bay (Brisbane), was the first administrator.

Holmes' place was taken by former convicts William Galvin, an Irish policeman transported for bayoneting a rioter, and John Roach, a London taxidermist convicted of stealing a coat.

The prospect of a natural history museum began taking shape in 1831. A committee of trustees appointed Dr George Bennett, an experienced naturalist, as curator, assisted by John Roach, the ex-taxidermist, when the museum opened to the public.

Bennett held the position till 1841 when the Reverend William Branwhite Clarke, sometimes known as the Father of Australian Geology, took on the job for two years.

In 1841 Clarke discovered gold in Hartley Valley but Governor Gipps, when shown a specimen in April 1844, exclaimed 'put it away Mr Clarke or we shall all have our throats cut'. When Clarke made it known after Gipps' death, the country did go a little mad and the Reverend Clarke was in demand. In 1851 he was commissioned to make a gold survey of NSW and located gold in parts of Victoria. He died in 1878 honoured for his work in Australia's geology.

In 1846 the Colonial Architect, Mortimer Lewis, began building the Australian Museum on its present site. Progress was slow those days; it took six years to complete.

German-born Johann Ludwig Gerrard Krefft, a skilled and zealous zoologist, was appointed acting curator in 1861. He was more at home with reptiles than with humans, a liability which later brought his demise. His work on Australian fauna and flora put him in touch with distinguished scientists Charles Darwin and Sir Reginald Owen. His expertise impressed the Trustees who made his position permanent after four years.

The Board of Trustees consisted of several influential men who were also keen collectors - sometimes using the Museum's facilities to further their private collections. Over the years Krefft became increasingly contemptuous of the Trustees, criticising their meanness and lack of understanding.

Conflict between curator and committee climaxed in December 1873 when gold specimens valued at £60 were stolen. The Trustees tried to implicate Krefft and the ensuing uproar resulted in the Legislative Assembly appointing a Select Committee into the operation of the Museum. Some trustees were included in the committee which meant sitting in judgment on themselves. Inevitably Krefft was dismissed but he refused to budge. Finally a trustee hired two prize fighters who forcibly ejected Krefft and his family from their living quarters in the Museum. Krefft himself was lifted out into the street stubbornly seated in his chair.

More than 2000 specimens loaned by the Museum to the International Exhibition were destroyed in the 1882 Garden Palace fire along with minerals and field notes belonging to the Reverend Clarke.

In the late 1880s the Museum staff had increased to eight and in 1893 the Technology Museum separated and moved into premises in Ultimo. An overseas visitor to the Museum wrote: 'The Sydney Museum is a noble building formed of the beautiful sandstone of the district. It is capacious, well lighted and remarkable for its cleanliness and order. Perhaps nowhere in Australia is there anything approaching the magnificent collection of Australian marsupial mammals here exhibited.'

In 1947 scores of butterfly specimens were found to be missing from the cabinets, some carefully replaced by paper replicas. Checks were made in the museums in Adelaide and Sydney where similar deficiencies totalled almost 3000. The culprit was soon recognised: an English butterfly expert named Colin Wyatt who had visited all three museums. He was arrested in London and the magistrate found that Wyatt had suffered from 'a temporary distraction of mind' and he was fined £100. Collectors can sometimes get carried away.

AROUND HYDE PARK 67

A view of the Australian Museum in College Street, from Hyde Park in the 1890s. (National Library of Australia)

Reproduced from the original Tyrrell Collection glass plate.

One Man's Bottleneck

In 1828 Surveyor-General, Thomas Mitchell was given the monumental task of surveying the colony of NSW. Land grants without clearly defined boundaries had been handed out with no attempt at a general survey.

Mitchell, who served under the Duke of Wellington as an officer-surveyor in the Peninsular Wars, proceeded, with inferior instruments, while tactfully avoiding confrontation with titleholders.

The South Head was approached along Old South Head Road (partly today's Oxford Street) and Mitchell's task was to plan a second road. Several fine villas occupied the Kings Cross area, some with Romanesque gardens descending to the Harbour foreshores.

Mitchell himself owned nine acres on which he built his elegant, two-storey Craigend. Anyone wishing to reach the area, then known as Woolloomooloo Heights, had to turn off Old South Head Road and follow the sand track which later became Darlinghurst Road.

Builders of the New South Head Road, starting with William Street, after reigning monarch William IV, were confronted at the top by sandhills. Curving the road around them meant bringing it into proximity to land belonging to Alexander Macleay's Elizabeth Bay House.

As Colonial Secretary, Macleay was second-in-command to Governor Darling. When William Street was under construction Surveyor Mitchell was away on a surveying expedition when the road was being built. It is said Macleay ordered the convict gang overseer to continue the road, with a slight curve, straight over the top. Mitchell was furious when he returned but it was too late. As a result the intersection at the top of William Street became a traffic bottleneck for almost 150 years. Not until December 1976, when the Kings Cross four-lane tunnel was punched through the hill to link William Street with Bayswater Road, was the problem solved.

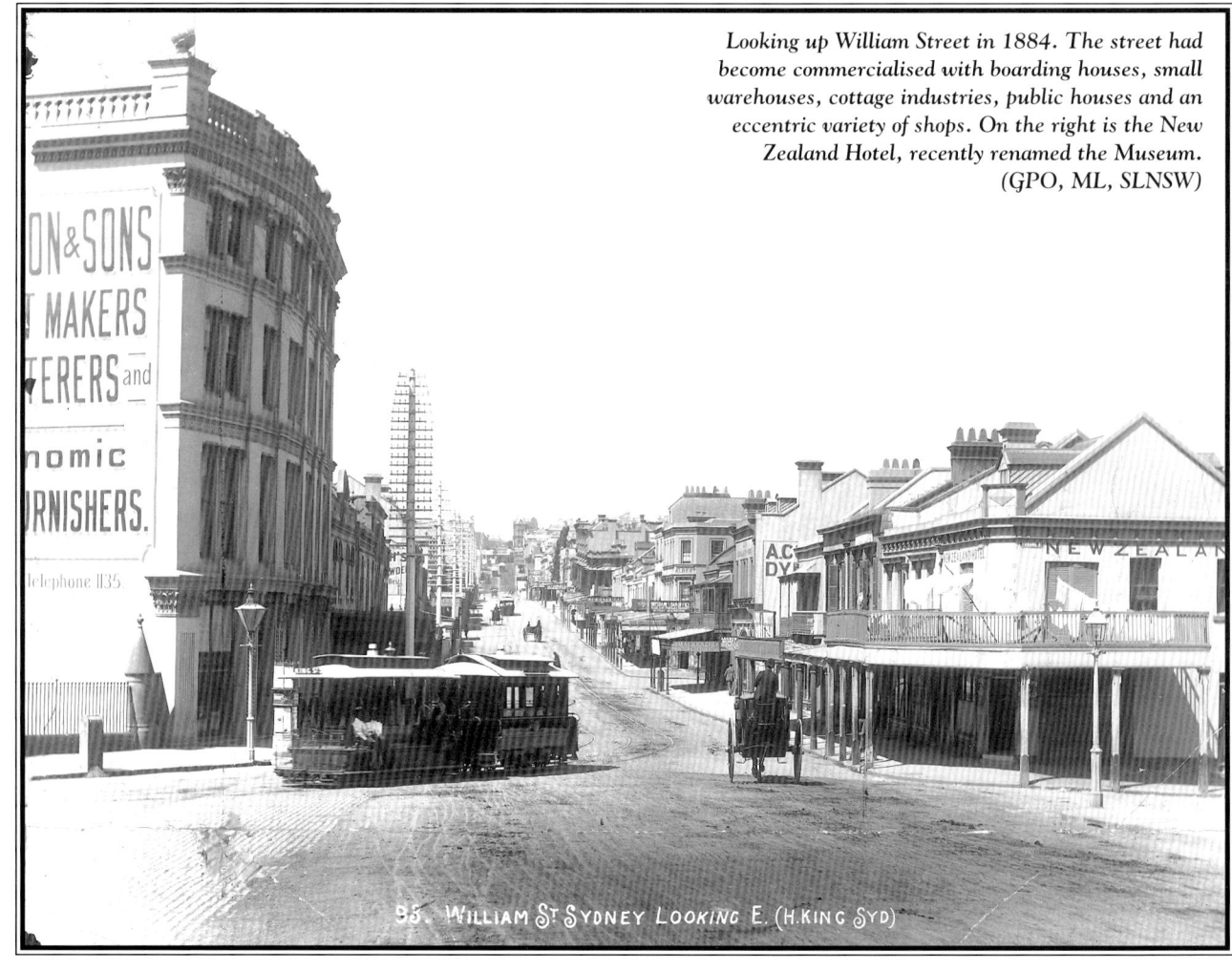

Looking up William Street in 1884. The street had become commercialised with boarding houses, small warehouses, cottage industries, public houses and an eccentric variety of shops. On the right is the New Zealand Hotel, recently renamed the Museum. (GPO, ML, SLNSW)

Jewish Genesis

There were at least eight known members of the Jewish faith among the convicts who arrived with the First Fleet; some 800 were transported over the entire convict era. The first free Jewish settler was the colourful Barnett Levey sometimes called The Father of Australian Theatre, who arrived to join his successful emancipist brother. Convicts of all denominations had to attend Church of England service every Sunday.

The first step towards an organised community was in 1817 when a small group of Jews got together to form a burial fund society. In July 1826 a Jewish couple, Phoebe Benjamin, silk glove maker, and Solomon Lyons, a weaver, were married before the Reverend Samuel Marsden in a Church of England ceremony at Parramatta. The happy couple had been transported for life for robbery. Because of the drastic shortage of females most young Jewish men took non-Jewish brides. Governor Darling was approached to provide accommodation for a congregation but the Governor ignored the request. On 8 August 1830 the *Sydney Gazette* reported:

All the Jews in Sydney and many from the country will meet at Messrs Cohen and Spyers in George Street who have kindly accommodated their brethren with the use of their large rooms as a temporary synagogue.

The rooms stood on the corner of Martin Plaza and George Street. The dissension between emancipists and free settlers prevailing in the general community was absent among the Jews because so many had convict associations.

In 1837 a two-storey building was rented on the north side of Bridge Street near the George Street corner but with an adult Jewish population close to 400, it was already too small. Four years later, president of the congregation, Moses Joseph, bought land in York Street, opposite the markets, for £1000. The synagogue was built in the height of the depression and the congregation had to turn to the Legislative Assembly to subsidise the construction cost of £3600. The building was described by the *Herald* as 'pleasing Egyptian' with three rows of open backed pews lit by two large gas chandeliers. When it opened in 1844 the din from the markets could be heard during the service.

A second synagogue opened in Macquarie Street opposite Parliament House in 1859. The two congregations combined in the Great Synagogue which opened in Elizabeth Street in March 1878, its magnificent interior accommodating 1600.

Today the Byzantine structure resolutely remains, pressed between lofty modern buildings, a persistent reminder of a more dignified age.

The Great Synagogue in Elizabeth Street seen from the Park Street corner in the 1890s. (National Library of Australia)

'No other store like David Jones'

'The customer is always right.' David Jones' Elizabeth Street store in 1932. (Home and Away, ML, SLNSW)

In Melbourne it was Myers in Sydney it was always David Jones. Ownership may have passed into other hands but the names are unshakeable. With a name like David Jones it's not a surprise the founder was a Welshman. At 18 he was managing a store and two years later he married. His wife died in childbirth and the young widower sought his fortune in London where he took several retailing positions and remarried. Through his new wife he met Charles Appleton, a Hobart Town businessman on a visit to London. Recognising Jones' ability and taken by his charm, Appleton offered him a partnership if he would come to Sydney. Appleton had opened a store in Pitt Street in 1825 and wanted Jones to manage it.

David Jones was 42 when he arrived to take up the position in September 1835. He began extending credit in the belief the needs of the customer came first. Turnover increased tenfold but Charles Appleton was appalled when he discovered Jones' 'reckless' credit policy. A violent argument came to blows and Jones was put on a bond for good behaviour.

David Jones opened his own store on the corner of George Street and Barrack Lane, opposite the General Post Office, in 1838 and a DJ's has occupied the site ever since. Each morning Jones welcomed customers at the door with a warm smile and a lilting Welsh greeting and many of Appleton's customers switched allegiances when he offered 'satisfaction or money back' years ahead of its time. The store survived the 1840s depression but almost failed to survive the retirement of its founder when Jones handed the business to his two new partners in the late 1850s. Within a short time the store faced closure. The aging merchandiser gave up his seat in parliament and returned to the store which was soon back on its feet. He finally did retire leaving the business to his son, Edward Lloyd Jones.

The eminent merchandiser died at his home in Lyons Terrace, Liverpool Street in March 1873, shortly after his eightieth birthday. I

Successive family members administered the store and in 1927 David Jones Elizabeth Street Store opened at a cost of £1 million, an amount which threatened company finances for years. A third store opened on the corner of Castlereagh and Market Streets in 1938.

In the changing world of the 1980s David Jones was taken over by the Adelaide Steamship Company and the family lost control of the business. The name remains: Sydney wouldn't be quite the same without it.

Sydney's 'Theatre Beautiful'

The extravagant picture palaces that animated the city in the 'sweet and twenties' were positively vulgar compared to the elegance of the Prince Edward. The 'Theatre Beautiful', almost opposite the Hotel Australia in Castlereagh Street, extended through to Elizabeth Street and was an eloquent salute to the silent movie era (talkies were three years away) when it opened on Saturday, 22 November 1924 with Cecil B. de Mille's *Ten Commandments*. Half of Sydney's population attended during the film's record three-year run.

It wasn't just the movie, it was the full 21-piece orchestra, raised and lowered on a hydraulic platform, and the £10 000 Wurlitzer organ that rose, with a musical gasp, from the stage depths.

Whereas the atmospheric cinemas sought to create the illusion of being in the open air, generous sprays of flowers, fresh from the markets, turned the chandelier-lit foyer into an enchanted grotto reverberating with the splash of the marble fountain. The plush auditorium with 1500 seats, upholstered in blue, rivalled those of a luxury hotel.

In 1964 rumours the Prince Edward had been sold to a developer were sadly confirmed. The final presentation was Tolstoy's *War and Peace* starring Audrey Hepburn and Henry Fonda on Saturday evening, 4 December 1965. Ironically the theatre just concluded its best box office year ever. The appearance of high-rise office blocks where the Prince Edward and the Hotel Australia once stood robbed that end of town of its sparkle.

The final weeks of the enchanting Prince Edward which had set new standards in cinema style and comfort.

Looking down Liverpool Street, bordering Hyde Park, from today's corner of College Street and Oxford Street. On the left hand side (with two trees growing in front of it) is Lyons Terrace. This elegant terrace was built in 1841 by John Verge and John Bibb for the Sydney auctioneer Samuel Lyons. The first terrace on the left was demolished in 1910 to make way for Wentworth Avenue. The next terrace made way for the Australian Picture Palace and the remaining two fell in 1923 to make way for the YWCA which is still situated in Wentworth Avenue. The Australian Picture Palace was later the site of the Paris Cinema.
(The Humphery Collection, National Library of Australia)

The Foy Boys

Palatial department stores seldom die, they simply fade away. Three department stores ruled the southern end of the city: Marcus Clarke's, Anthony Hordern's and Mark Foy's. Like the period in which they were built, their splendour and stability seemed everlasting. Although some tried to adapt, they were overwhelmed by history and 60 years after they opened in a blaze of glory they vanished, leaving memories clinging to merchandise bought there.

Francis Foy and his younger brother, Mark Foy junior, arrived in Sydney in 1885 and two years later opened Mark Foy's Drapery Palace, named after their late father. Mark Foy senior had owned a drapery store in the Melbourne suburb of Collingwood and handed the business to Francis who brought in a partner, William Gibson. The partnership was dissolved although Foy and Gibson's store continued trading in Melbourne.

The Foy brothers' Oxford Street drapery was so successful they built a more ambitious store, modelled on Bon Marche of Paris, on the corner of Elizabeth and Liverpool Street in 1908. Its towers became a city landmark and its marble shopping halls, illuminated by lavish chandeliers, were seen to offer the most fashionable merchandise in Sydney. Patrons could ride the city's first escalator to the ballroom or take afternoon tea on the piazza.

Irish-born Francis Foy arrived in Victoria as a child becoming something of a wild colonial boy in his youth. He remained a colourful personality all his life. Always generous in private life he was admonished for working his shop girls a 52-hour week in the late 1890s, when stores opened till 11 pm six days a week. Francis was a well-known turf identity importing horses from Britain; his Melbourne Cup champagne lunches were legendary. He suffered from diabetes and always the betting man bet his bookie three to one he would not return alive from a visit to the 1918 Melbourne Cup. He died on the Melbourne-Sydney express just outside Goulburn, on his way home.

Changing transport patterns, influenced by the city railway and the Harbour Bridge, impaired trading but Foy's considered themselves lucky when a subway linked the store entrance with the new Museum Station. Two storeys were added to the building and trading peaked in 1928-29 but as city shopping became centralised the southern end became increasingly isolated.

Mark Foy junior, whose interests lay in sailing and motoring, opened the Hydro Majestic Hotel in Medlow Bath in the Blue Mountains in 1904, bringing in a Swiss doctor and spa water from Baden Baden in Germany. He died at his home in Bayview on Sydney's northern beaches at the ripe age of 95 in 1950 before witnessing the decline and closure of the store bearing his and his father's name.

The forecourt at Mark Foys on the Elizabeth, Liverpool Street corner, seen here in 1932, became Sydney's first outdoor cafeteria with a Parisian touch.

Hunter Street
'An Excellent Site'

'Throughout its whole extent Hunter Street is an excellent site; several of its frontages being occupied as town residences of gentlemen of the first respectability,' wrote James Maclehose in his *Picture of Sydney* in 1848. It remains an excellent site, a mixture of new commercial buildings and a few obstinate old ones. A gentleman's residence with a fine garden and iron gates, on the south-west corner of Pitt and Hunter Street, belonged to wealthy merchant Richard 'China' Jones. Later the Currency Lass Hotel, a favourite with gold miners in town in the 1850s, occupied the site. O'Farrell, the Irish agitator who attempted to assassinate the Duke of Edinburgh in 1868, lodged here. The opposite corner is still referred to as the *Herald* Corner although the newspaper moved to Broadway decades before.

In the 1840s many residences gave way to tradespeople 'whose stores and shops,' according to a visitor, 'are fully equal to those of a principal street in an English city'.

The street was named in honour of John Hunter, the second governor (1795-1800). It dipped from George Street to the Tank Stream valley and up again and was, with its little bridge, the only cross street between Bridge and King streets until Martin Place opened up in the 1890s. As cross streets go, Bridge Street became self-important; King Street was always candy-striped and companionable; Market Street in disarray but Hunter Street was, like its namesake, a trifle pompous.

In a double-fronted cottage on the north side of the street, just down from Macquarie Street, lived a pious hypocrite named John Tawell, whom his opposite neighbour, Judge Therry, described as wearing a 'broad-brimmed hat' and a 'neat and carefully adjusted costume' giving the impression of a 'very saintly personage'.

Tawell, who arrived in 1815 for passing a forged banknote, was a Quaker and an apothecary (chemist) who achieved wealth and respectability in the colony. To prove his sincerity he once poured 600 gallons of spirits into the Harbour. Unexpectedly his wife and sons followed him to Sydney where he was living with his mistress. Both boys later died of fever. Grief stricken, Tawell and his wife returned to England where she became ill. A compulsive womaniser, Tawell formed a liaison with her nurse by whom he had two children.

On the death of his wife he remarried. Fearing his new wife might discover his affair, he called on his mistress at her cottage near Windsor in Berkshire, and put poison in her drink. Leaving the body he took the London train but the murder was quickly discovered and a telegraph was sent ahead to London where he was arrested at the train station. It was the first time telegraphy was used to catch a criminal. Tawell confessed his guilt and was executed in March 1845. Apart from the northern side of King Street, no Sydney street has altered so completely as Hunter Street.

Facing Hunter Street from Macquarie Street in the 1890s. The old cottage on the right was once occupied by John Tawell, the poisoning apothecary.

*Hunter Street from the George Street corner.
No city street has seen so much change.
(National Library of Australia)*

The *Herald's* Birthplace

Three young men, all in their twenties, two of whom were employed by the *Sydney Gazette*, imported a press and opened a printing shop. Business was slow so they decided to publish an independent newspaper. It was a bold move; three newspapers were already appearing in Sydney. Their four-page weekly *Sydney Herald* first came out 18 April 1831.

It was produced from a two-storey building in Redman Court behind the Keep within Compass Inn, on the east side of Lower George Street facing Essex Street. Within six months they were printing more copies than their three competitors combined. In 1838, with the colony desperately short of compositors, a notice appeared:

Wanted six compositors at the HERALD office. To emigrants of sober habit and good workmen constant employment will be given. Wages from 40/- to 60/- per week. None need apply who are in the habit of working two days a week and being drunk the other four.

That year saw the colony's first industrial dispute when *Sydney Herald* compositors demanded a wage increase from two pounds two shillings a week to two pounds eight shillings a week. Management finally gave in but the strike leaders were sacked soon after.

Two of the partners sold their interest and the *Sydney Herald* was left in the hands of Frederick Stokes who eventually sold it to Charles Kemp, one of his employees, in partnership with John Fairfax, a former English provincial newspaper owner. Now titled the *Sydney Morning Herald* the publication took up residence in new premises on the corner of Pitt and Hunter Streets and eventually became one of the most prestigious newspapers in the British Commonwealth.

When the first *Herald* building was demolished in 1916, a small stone jetty with two flights of stairs was uncovered well below the level of George Street, a reminder of the days when the waters of the cove lapped the lower end of Pitt Street as far as Bridge Street.

The *Herald* remained in the Fairfax family for 150 years until a family member, Warwick Fairfax Junior, borrowed $2 billion in a takeover bid but lost control when he defaulted on the debt.

The Herald Corner without the Herald in 1964.

The *Herald* Corner

John Fairfax, former owner of an English provincial newspaper, arrived with his wife and three children and £5 in his pocket in 1838. His decision to begin a new life followed a lawsuit which left him penniless. Printers were scarce in the colony and he soon found work as a compositor. His knowledge of books and his obvious integrity won him librarianship of the Australian Subscription Library. Being one of the few intellectual amenities in the colony it put him in touch with several leading citizens, among them the proprietor of the *Sydney Herald*, Frederick Stokes. To augment his modest salary Fairfax worked part time for the *Herald* and was soon offered the full-time position of manager which he declined.

It was all too much for Stokes when the paper went daily so he sold it to his political reporter in partnership with John Fairfax for £10 000 on extended credit. The partnership lasted 12 years in which time 'Morning' was added to the title. Kemp sold his share to Fairfax who brought his son Charles into the business.

The colony underwent rapid change in the gold rush years of the 1850s, the population increasing by almost one million, with *Herald* sales rising accordingly. The Lower George Street premises were too small and Fairfax purchased a triangular block of land on the north-east corner of Pitt and Hunter Street where an ancient cottage stood on the site. Here Fairfax built an Italianate, three-storey home for his expanding newspaper. The first headline published from the new offices on 30 June 1856 announced 'Glorious News from Europe' the end of the Crimean War, an event, in those pre-cable years, which had taken place three months earlier.

The *Herald* providing 'an impartial stage for the discussion of questions of public interest' grew in size and importance. When John Fairfax died in 1877 he had seen his modest newspaper develop into one of the most respected English-speaking dailies.

In July 1929 a new *Herald* building was completed on the site with the head of William Caxton, the first English printer, over the front door, the sole relic from the original premises.

During the Depression years, job seekers gathered at the *Herald* Corner in the early hours to catch the edition hot off the press. There was little to choose from on Saturday, 17 December 1932 when the list of jobs available had shrunk to two-and-a-half columns.

One hundred years after first occupying the site, the *Herald* landmark disappeared from the city centre when the offices and equipment moved to Jones Street, Broadway. It was 1956 and the appearance and personality of the city's centre was about to undergo enormous change.

The old Herald *offices on the corner of Pitt and Hunter Streets in the 1930s. (John Fairfax and Sons)*

Pitt Street puzzle 1851: the centre tree marks the junction of Pitt and Spring Streets; to the left of the tree buildings occupy the site of the future Royal Exchange. The Herald building was erected on the site of the cottages on the right foreground. The Tank Stream on the left flows down to Sydney Cove with a view of the stone bridge at Bridge Street.
(Royal Australian Historical Society)

Pitt Street Horse Power

Shortly after 6 am, two days before Christmas 1861, Sydney's first tramcar came trundling along Pitt Street from Circular Quay. The few people in the street paused to gape, some even waved to passengers on the roof, as the huge, canary yellow carriage drawn by four horses rolled past.

The government saw the tramway as a cheap alternative to a branch line from the rail terminus to the wharves at Circular Quay. Residents and shopkeepers were against having half their narrow thoroughfare taken up with rails but the Bill got through the Legislative Assembly and two tramcars arrived in the *Marcianus* in July 1861.

Each carriage carried 30 passengers 'on comfortable cushioned seats' inside the saloon car and an iron ladder led to the roof where another 30 passengers could sit either side of the centre bench. The two mile trot from the Quay to the railhead took ten minutes, passengers reported the ride 'extremely easy' compared to the 'rattling and jolting' of the horse omnibus.

The tramcars were each named Old England and Young Australia, both bore the message 'Unity is the strength of nations' with a lion and eagle emblem. A few months later the driver of Old England, Mr Patrick, came before the court for 'driving too fast and recklessly' - a euphemism for drunkenness.

The rails protruded above the level of the street and carriages and carts received a nasty jolt every time they crossed. The 'carriage trade' began avoiding Pitt Street to the consternation of the shopkeepers. Those using the Pitt Street horse tramway may have found it convenient but its critics were highly vocal.

In January 1864 the Australia's first composer, Isaac Nathan, was killed when he stepped from the tram at Goulburn Street. The tramway was already ridiculed by the press and the incident provided fuel for those who wanted it removed.

Following a parliamentary debate at the end of 1866, the Tramway Bill was repealed even though some Pitt Street merchants had come to terms with the trams.

The last Pitt Street horse tram ran the last day of 1866. Next day removal of the rails began and four horse omnibuses took over the route. It was almost 13 years before Sydney saw trams back in the streets only this time horsepower was replaced by steam power.

A Pitt Street horse tram waits on the Hunter Street corner in the 1860s. One of the original cars was in use as a shed in the railway yards in World War I. (Public Transport Commission of NSW)

Christmas at Woolworth's

Percy Christmas was not the first man whose life was changed by a book - only in Percy's case the wrong book turned out to be the right one. It was titled *The Clock Without Hands* and he bought it believing it was a mystery story; it turned out to be essays on advertising.

Early last century advertising had become an integral part of retailing and Percy, a commercial traveller, took a correspondence course in it. He opened a blouse and hosiery shop in the Queen Victoria Building in partnership with a former floor manager at David Jones. Boosted by mail order advertising and their catchcry 'No Shop Rent', falsely implying prices must be cheaper, business expanded and in 1924 they sought larger premises.

They found new premises in a basement in the Imperial Arcade, opposite Hordern Brothers, in Pitt Street. Rent was cheap but the basement was too sombre for displaying ladies wear and they decided to offer a wide range of low cost merchandise. The American chain store company, F.W. Woolworths, was already established and as it had no plans to enter the Australian market, Christmas was allowed to use the name minus the 'F.W'.

'Woolworth's Stupendous Bargain Basement' opened three weeks before Christmas 1924. It was preceded by an advertising campaign with the slogan: 'Every price a cut price.' The store was an immediate success. In 1928 a second store opened in Pitt and ran through to Market Street.

'Father' Christmas, as he was inevitably known to his staff, was particular in his choice of shop assistants sometimes sending them to a phrenologist before allowing them to wear the red and white Woolworth's uniform. In 1928 a junior stock clerk named Theo Kelly joined the company. Years later he would preside over a multi-million dollar retail empire.

Percy Christmas, the former 'Shore' student and one-time travelling salesman, who bought the wrong book which led to the right business, died in 1947 when a Woolworth's store was represented in most major suburbs and towns across the country.

The store between the corners of Pitt and Market Streets remained in this location until its demolition to make way for the Centrepoint Tower and shopping arcade.

Woolworth's Stupendous Bargain Basement in Pitt Street, in the basement of the Imperial Arcade, when it opened for Christmas 1924.

Her Majesty's Theatre in Pitt Street lasted 15 years before it was destroyed by fire. The arcade which ran from Pitt to Castlereagh kept the name alive.

'Let's All Go Down the Strand'

On 1 April 1892 four hundred guests attended the opening of the Strand Arcade, Sydney's fifth, most ambitious arcade linking George and Pitt Streets. They came to admire the little 18th century type shops, to gaze up at the cantilevered galleries and to marvel at the chandeliers - each carrying fifty jets of gas and fifty electric lamps. Electricity was a novelty and so too was the city's first fruit salad shop where one enjoyed a fresh bowl topped with icing sugar or paused for a cup of tea or coffee at Harris's, the only original shop still open a hundred years later.

The Strand Arcade replaced the White Horse Tavern at the George Street end, its notoriety dated from the days prize-fighter Larry Foley taught boxing in a rear annex.

The Strand, located close to the hub of the city, was the most popular of the Sydney arcades which began changing or disappearing in the 1960s, their Victorian charm replaced by sleek glass and coloured concrete.

Fortunately the Prudential Assurance Company took over the Strand Arcade in 1974. Two years later the arcade was gutted by fire but the company had the resources to restore it to its original opulence. Today the Strand Arcade has recaptured the shine and the warmth of its Victorian original with the central staircase and a brass gas lamp.

The Royal Arcade, between Pitt and George Streets, in 1892. The site is now occupied by the Hilton Hotel. Unlike the Strand, this unique, roofless arcade failed to survive the development of the city. Who remembers the other arcades which cut between the main streets like decorated alleyways - the Piccadilly, the Sydney, the old Her Majesty's, the Imperial, Hordern's and the Hunter?

Pitt Street, from King Street.

Pitt Street: Sydney's Grand Canyon

More than any thoroughfare, Pitt Street typifies Sydney's brash, outgoing personality. Once it was a slumberous valley with a sparkling rivulet into which water dribbled from the swamp flats of Hyde Park until heavy rain sent it surging down to Sydney Cove.

It was first known as Pitt's Row said to be in honour of British Prime Minister, Sir William Pitt, although it is unlikely the dusty, disreputable track would be named after so distinguished a personage. It is suggested the name derives from the pits dug for fresh water in the bed of the Tank Stream.

Pitt Street played second fiddle to the haughtier High Street - which became George Street in 1810 - developing in spurts from a line of flapping tents beside the Tank Stream. It finally attained full length in the 1860s when the Tank Stream, by then little more than an open sewer, disappeared underground from Bridge Street to Sydney Cove.

Pitt Street's first tie-up with the tram, once an intrinsic part of Sydney life, began in 1861 when a horse tramway ran its length for several years. There was no stopping the horseless steam trams which began barging through in the 1880s, pursuing hapless pedestrians and playing havoc with the horses.

Trams, with their fearsome clatter and clanging bells, dominated Pitt Street for 70 years. Crammed knee to knee in carriage compartments, passengers could window shop from a seated position and during frequent traffic jams even lean out and purchase a dozen peaches from a fruit barrow at the side of the road.

There was always something to look at even if it was the footpath with its sea of preoccupied faces. The trams were plucked off Pitt Street in the late 1950s in preparation, it seemed, for Pitt Street to catch up with the multi-storey blocks which were taking over Sydney's skyline.

Even the antiquated Royal Arcade disappeared beneath the ugly splendour of the Hilton Hotel which graciously chose to accommodate the famous Marble Bar when Adams Hotel was demolished in 1969. It was here artists sank schooners in company with cartoonists and authors down from the Blue Mountains caught up with newspaper cobbers. Today computer men and share brokers drop into the dim bars for a gin and tonic or a Hahn beer.

Pitt Street has lost its down-at-heel look especially since the Pitt Street Mall opened in September 1987. Unlike King Street, rendered impotent by granite blocks and towering glass, Pitt Street has hung on to its personality, self-assured, somewhat impudent, still scruffy in places, a street that could only be found in a city like Sydney.

Narrow Pitt Street from King Street, crammed with people and traffic, looking south towards Market Street, in 1912. Note the Strand Arcade on the right.

A Sydney Site: Pitt & Market

The name Centrepoint could not be more appropriate for this nexus of commerce and human traffic in the centre of the city. The following pages contain a series of photographs showing the enormous changes this intersection has seen in less than a hundred years.

Many hotels have graced the site, in 1855 the Centrepoint corner was the location of the Australia Hotel, across the road was the Cricketers Arms, on the Myers corner David Bell the draper clothed gentlemen and across the road was the Exhibition Hotel.

This corner remained the site of hotels for the next century, and the draper was replaced for the next 25 years by an hotel before the arrival of Farmers and Company with fine furnishings, quality clothing and manchester.

With the opening of Her Majesty's Theatre in Pitt Street in 1887 this intoxicating location sobered up. The Australian Banking Company moved in to the ground floor of the five storey George Hotel in Market Street, next door to the theatre, and across the road the London Chartered Bank opened for trading in the 1880s.

From the single storey butcher shop in 1869 rose the Centrepoint Tower, from the draper's came the 12 storey Farmers. Sydney was on the up and up even in 1887, demolishing its past to make way for a bigger and brighter future.

The north east corner of Pitt and Market Streets as it was in the 1870s: B. Byrne's butcher shop had prime spot on the corner; next door Murton and Sheridan provided surgery, dentistry and drugs; Bland's sold supper for sixpence; then came Woodward, an oyster merchant; F.C. Kirkby sold music, periodicals, theatrical books and magazines from overseas; J.P. Hamilton was an auctioneer; and a few doors down was the Civil Service Co-operative of New South Wales building which survived in this spot past 1902. These establishments were demolished to make way for Her Majesty's theatre in 1887. (SPF, ML, SLNSW)

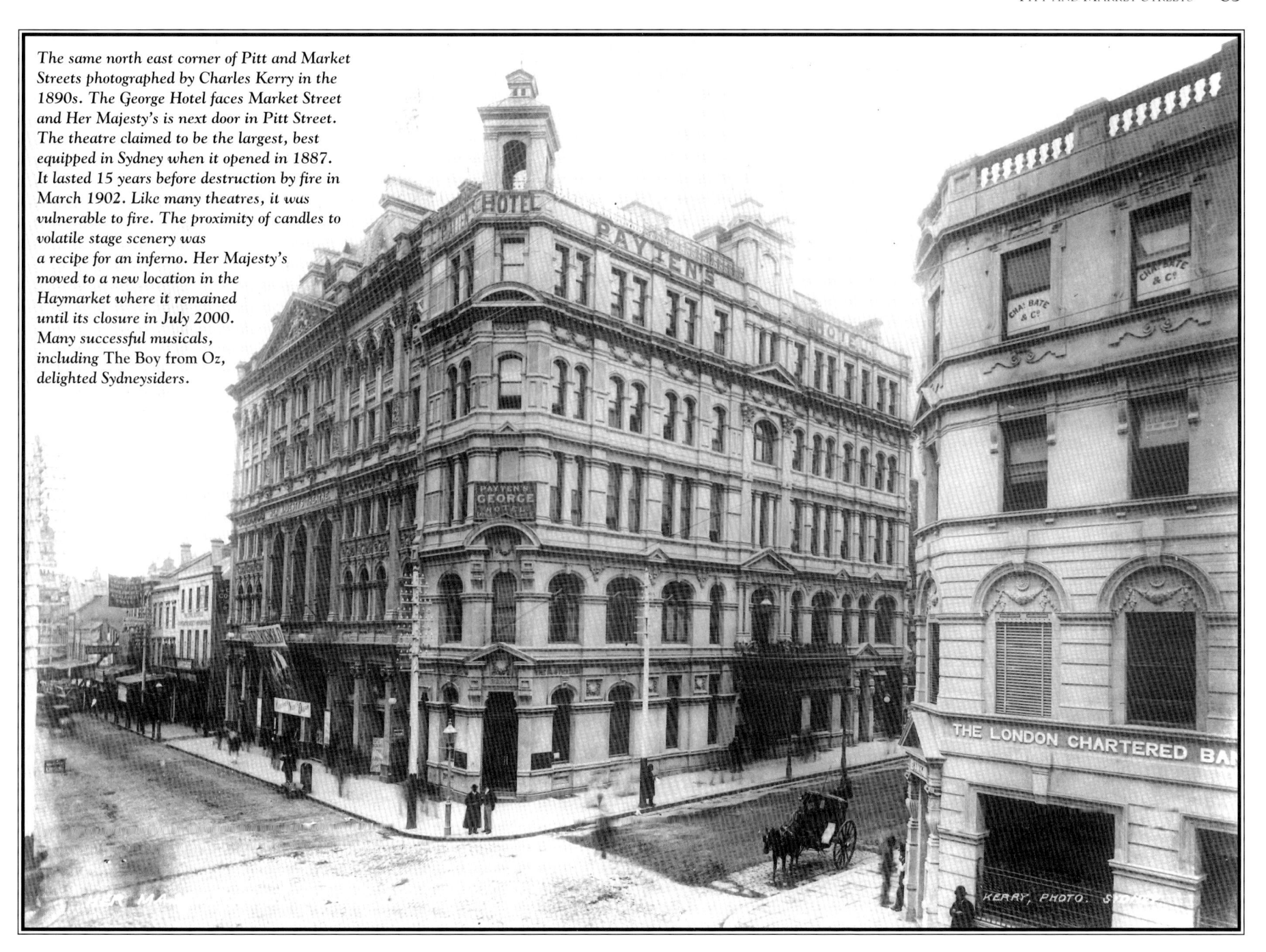

The same north east corner of Pitt and Market Streets photographed by Charles Kerry in the 1890s. The George Hotel faces Market Street and Her Majesty's is next door in Pitt Street. The theatre claimed to be the largest, best equipped in Sydney when it opened in 1887. It lasted 15 years before destruction by fire in March 1902. Like many theatres, it was vulnerable to fire. The proximity of candles to volatile stage scenery was a recipe for an inferno. Her Majesty's moved to a new location in the Haymarket where it remained until its closure in July 2000. Many successful musicals, including The Boy from Oz, delighted Sydneysiders.

Farmers: 'A Cut Above'

His name was Farmer and he was a farmer but became a draper after he arrived in Sydney and opened a shop opposite the Royal Victoria Theatre in Pitt Street. Joseph and Caroline Farmer were assisted immigrants in their mid-twenties for whom Australia proved a land of opportunity. They opened for business, near the Imperial Arcade in Pitt Street in 1840 and moved across the street to larger premises as business flourished. The store boomed through the gold rush years and in 1854 the couple decided to retire, handing the business to their nephew William who took a series of partners as the business grew.

The store's grand Victoria House, was built in 1873 on part of what became the Pitt Street end of the modern store and featured a granite colonnade and the colony's first large plate glass windows. It was also the first department store to introduce weekend closing after Saturday lunchtime when retail staff usually worked till 11 pm six days a week. Farmers' prices were usually a cut above everyone else's which gave the store its snooty reputation. According to one long-time employee: 'The cheapest shirt in the store used to be one guinea - anywhere else in Sydney, five shillings!'

Farmer and Co. became a limited company in 1897 and the old Victoria House building was demolished 13 years later to make way for expansion around from Pitt Street and along Market Street. The pub on the corner of Market and George Streets was destroyed by fire in 1918 and Farmers acquired the site and built its 12-storey extension. In 1922 Australia's first radio station was established in the store with the call sign 2FC, later taken over by the ABC.

The site of the George Street end of the store was once occupied by a town house belonging to the Blaxland family (Gregory was one of the three explorers who crossed the Blue Mountains) and the store established the Blaxland Gallery, near the roof garden, in his memory.

The store reached its peak in the postwar years by keeping ahead of the changes in marketing. In November 1960 the company accepted the offer of a merger from the Myer Emporium of Melbourne. Sixteen years later, with the stroke of a boardroom pen, the Farmers' name, familiar to Sydney shoppers for 136 years, disappeared.

The north west corner of Pitt and Market Streets showing Farmers' Victoria House store in 1882. This building was demolished in 1910. The post office tower is in the background.

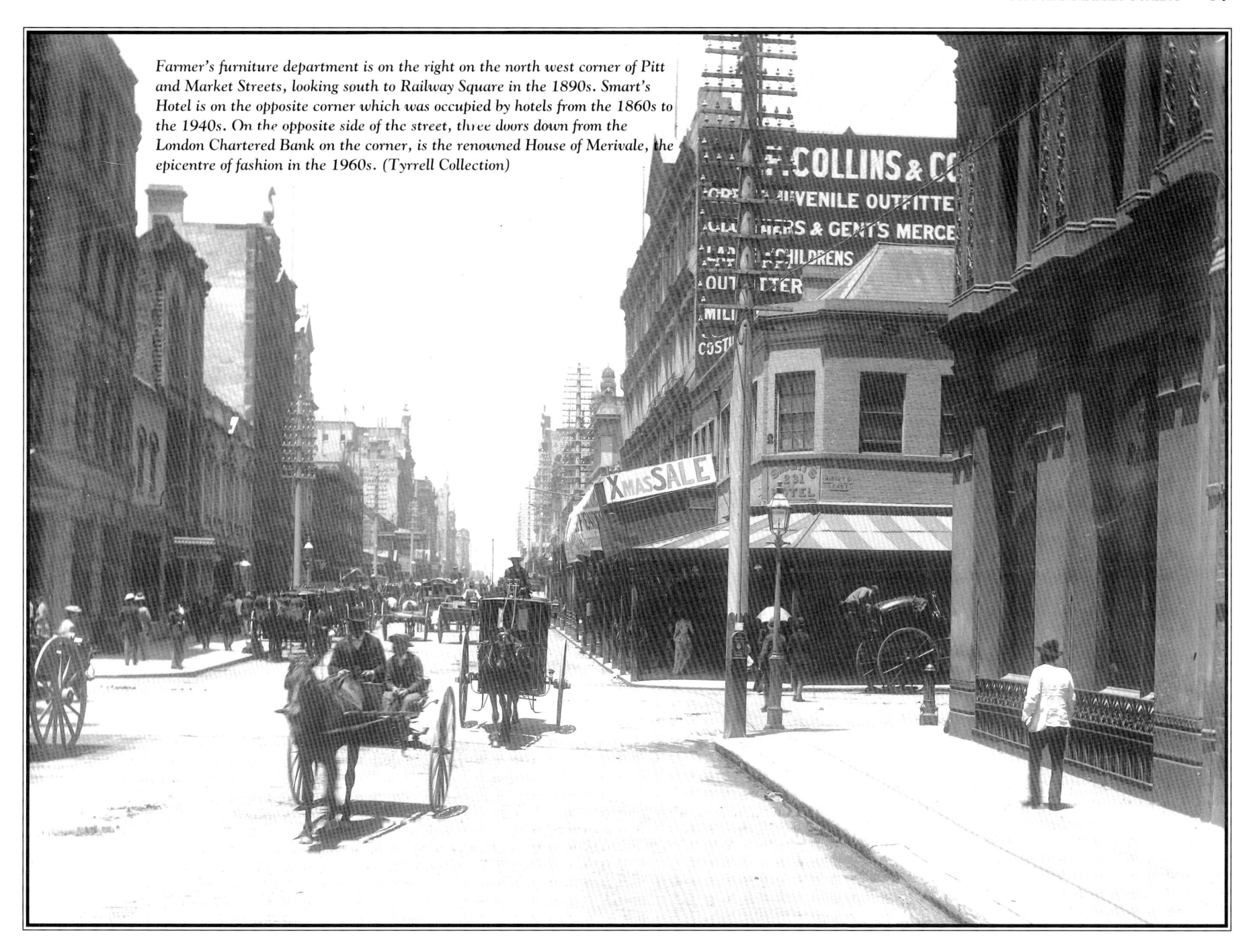

Farmer's furniture department is on the right on the north west corner of Pitt and Market Streets, looking south to Railway Square in the 1890s. Smart's Hotel is on the opposite corner which was occupied by hotels from the 1860s to the 1940s. On the opposite side of the street, three doors down from the London Chartered Bank on the corner, is the renowned House of Merivale, the epicentre of fashion in the 1960s. (Tyrrell Collection)

88   Pitt and Market Streets

The commercial corner of Pitt and Market Streets in 1932 looking towards King Street. The caped policeman has halted the traffic to let anxious jaywalkers fill the street. Pitt Street was almost a mall in those days.

Pitt Street between King and Market Streets looking south in 1940. Note the barrow at the side of the road selling fruit. (John Fairfax and Son)

The Stately State

'Its stunningly extravagant decor stands as a monument to that foolish and fabulous decade, the 1920s' announced the National Trust when it gave the State Theatre an 'A' classification in 1973. The classification is reserved for buildings of great historical significance or high architectural quality.

On Saturday, 8 June 1929, the Sydney press was unanimous in its praise of the magnificent new picture theatre in Market Street. The glittering opening occurred the previous evening in the presence of the Governor-General, Lord Stonehaven, the Governor of NSW, Sir Dudley De Chair and NSW Premier Tom Bavin.

Stuart Doyle, head of Greater Union Theatres added a cultural touch with a multiplicity of sculptures and vases and a mezzanine art gallery. Instead of a star-studded 'sky' the elaborate plasterwork was illuminated by a dazzling 20 000 piece chandelier and instead of heading off to the 'Gents' one entered the Pioneer Room, complete with its pair of muskets, while the 'Ladies' tripped off to the Butterfly Room.

Those who could afford the price of a box office ticket felt like royalty. The feeling was not shared by Greater Union Theatres who acquired mammoth bank loans to finance their entertainment palace but the company held on through the depressed 1930s until the movie industry's good times were back with World War II. It was from the ten-storey State block Norman B. Rydge, who took over chairmanship from Stuart Doyle in 1937, published *Rydge's Business Journal* which he introduced in 1928.

Since it was refurbished in the early 1980s, the State Theatre has never looked more regal. Having survived its first 50 years without so much as a coat of paint and having won the ultimate accolade, the Builders' Labourers' Federation 'green ban', it seems the State is here to stay.

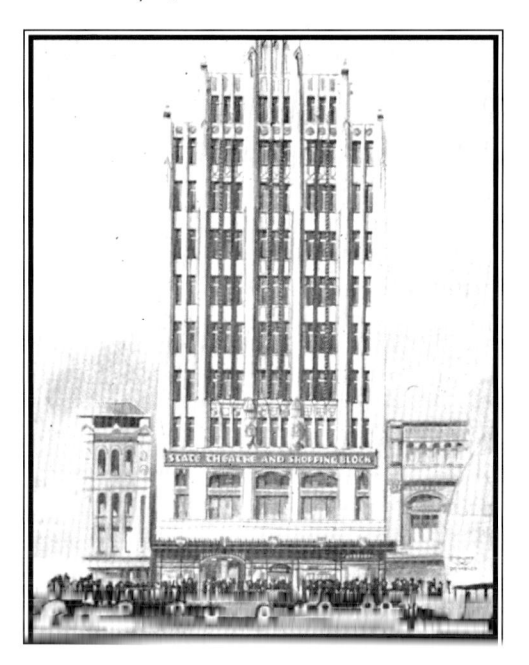

The grand foyer at the State Theatre in 1978.
(John Fairfax & Sons)

An artist's drawing of the State Theatre in 1929.

Martin Place in the late 1880s before the great fire which gutted the whole block bordered by Pitt and Castlereagh streets.

Flower sellers in Martin Place during World War I. (National Library of Australia)

Martin Place in the late 1880s, before the enormous fire which destroyed all the buildings seen in the centre of the photograph in Castlereagh Street. The fire began in the printing works of the Illustrated Sydney News on the 2 October 1890. It destroyed the entire city block bordered by Pitt, Castlereagh, Moore Streets and Hosking Place and opened the extension of Martin Place across Castlereagh Street. Photographed by Charles Kerry.
(National Library of Australia)

A Place Called Martin Plaza

London has Piccadilly, New York Times Square and Sydney has Martin Plaza which some will call 'Martin Place' till the day they die. Martin Plaza, located squarely among the power citadels, government, banks and insurance companies, that make a city tick, is the scene of historic events and private memories, some as elusive as sweet-scented boronias on the flower stalls. To the credit of some Town Hall visionaries, Martin Place, or Plaza, became a space for people to congregate, communicate or cogitate over a lunch-hour sandwich.

The majestic plaza began life as an anonymous laneway squeezed between shabby shopfronts and the grand post office building in George Street. The shops were brushed aside, replaced by a broad thoroughfare reaching to Pitt Street. Narrow Moore Street, ran from there up to Castlereagh Street.

Hereabouts one George Crossley lived. Crossley was, in modern terms, a 'bent lawyer' his shady career in 18th century London ceased when he entered Newgate Gaol en route to Botany Bay. Even in Sydney he was in trouble. The story goes he put a fly in the mouth of a dead man and guided his hand to trace a signature.

At his trial he claimed the will had been signed by the deceased 'while there was life in him'. Crossley's mansion was later occupied by John Hosking, first mayor of Sydney, who married the daughter of rich emancipist Sam Terry. Later it became the Metropolitan Hotel which was gutted in the great fire of 1890.

The fire began in the printing works of Gibbs, Shallard and Company, publishers of the *Illustrated Sydney News*, at three in the morning of 2 October. It destroyed an entire city block bounded by Pitt, Castlereagh, Moore Street and Hosking Place but it opened the extension of Martin Place through to Castlereagh Street.

In February 1891, the street was given its name in honour of the late Chief Justice, Sir James Martin, although the Moore Street name stuck till 1923. Twelve years later the extension to Macquarie Street completed Martin Place.

Sydney's posh Prince's Restaurant opened at number 42 in December 1938. Among Sydney's 'cafe society' in attendance was youthful, debonair Gough Whitlam, who was to become Australia's Prime Minister.

Almost as famous as the cenotaph was the subterranean 'Gents' in the middle of the street. Above it ticked one of the most dependable clocks in Sydney: 'The Watch on the U-Rhine' it was called adding the 'U' to the title of a well-known play. The clock stands at Warringah Mall, near Manly, still keeping perfect time. Another clock topped the GPO tower. Both clock and tower were dismantled in 1942 because it was feared that it was a landmark for Japanese air attack. Someone overlooked the Harbour Bridge!

Outside the Commonwealth Bank on the south-east Pitt Street corner, former World War I Prime Minister, Billy Hughes, stood every Anzac Day to salute returned servicemen from two world wars.

The Eastern Suburbs Railway was envisaged about the time the first stage of the GPO was completed in 1874. A disused tunnel, the start of the railway, was left forgotten beneath Martin Place for a hundred years. One day, late in 1979, Sydneysiders awoke to find the long-standing joke that was the Eastern Suburbs Railway had become a reality.

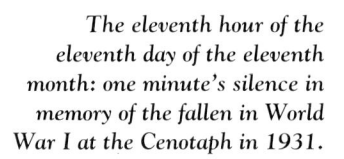

The eleventh hour of the eleventh day of the eleventh month: one minute's silence in memory of the fallen in World War I at the Cenotaph in 1931.

Jubilation in Martin Place when news of the 1918 Armistice was received and men of the first AIF would soon be home. (John Fairfax and Sons)

The Grand Post Office

A disorderly George Street bordered with orderly Victorian public buildings which survived the demolition mania of the last 50 years.

In 1809 impostors were boarding overseas vessels claiming mail that wasn't theirs. The man chosen to solve the problem was, Isaac Nichols, assistant to the Port Naval Officer a diligent ex-convict who became Australia's first postmaster. All incoming mail had to be collected, from his whitewashed cottage in George Street just up from Sydney Cove.

Nichols, a semi-literate country boy, had been sentenced to seven years' transportation for stealing a donkey. He arrived in Sydney in 1791 and the industrious young man caught the attention of Governor Hunter who made him chief overseer of the Sydney convict work gangs. When his sentence expired the Governor granted him 50 acres at Concord with two assigned convicts to work the land.

In March 1799 Nichols was sentenced to 14 years on Norfolk Island for receiving stolen property. Overseers were despised and Governor Hunter, recognising a conspiracy, referred the matter to London where it was pigeon-holed for two years before the order came for Nichols' release. Years later, when Nichols built his own ship, he named it the Governor Hunter.

Governor Macquarie found Nichols 'zealous, active and useful' and gave him more land and a spirit licence. Nichols entered the coastal trade and eventually died a rich man in 1819. In his will the former illiterate countryman paid for his sons to be educated in England.

In 1828 the post office moved into the police station building, the site of what became the GPO, in George Street. In November 1838 the Postmaster-General, James Raymond, introduced prepaid postage for letters delivered within the Sydney area, a world first.

A post office in keeping with the growing importance of the colony was planned and additional land was acquired from the Terry family. The Colonial Architect, James Barnet, designed an Italian Renaissance sandstone structure with a colonnade, stepped up from the footpath, along one side. It was to be the grandest building in Australia.

It took 21 years from 1866 to complete; the clock tower was added in 1891. The GPO created as much controversy as the Sydney Opera House did almost a century later. During construction the post office operated from 'temporary' premises in Wynyard Square. for ten years

The GPO was built in stages, the foundation for the Pitt Street extension was laid in 1881. Barnet included an effigy of himself among the mini sculptures of artists and scientists portrayed in stone above the arches at the Pitt Street entrance. The newspapers considered them grotesque and public agitation almost brought Barnet undone. The George Street section was ready for occupation on 1 September 1874 with 1500 citizens at the opening to marvel at Sydney's first electric lift. Premier Sir Henry Parkes was doubtful whether the interior was functional for its purpose; later it was extensively altered.

In 1942 the landmark GPO clock and tower were removed for fear of Japanese bombs. In spite of the postwar jibes it was finally restored in 1964. In the 1990s the interior was completely redesigned for use as a first-class hotel.

The General Post Office and Martin Place at the turn of the century, almost a decade after its completion and after the fourth floor was added. The French attics on either end of the building were added to accommodate the telephone exchange and the operators. (Australia Post Archives)

Unique Rowe Street

The changing face of the city robbed Rowe Street of its unique charm. The street (originally named Brougham Place) ran from Pitt Street to Castlereagh Street just south of Martin Plaza. It was really a laneway, named after architect Thomas Rowe who designed the Great Synagogue, Sydney Hospital in Macquarie Street and Newington College in Stanmore.

The Hotel Australia, at the Castlereagh Street end, breathed life into the darkened, narrow street in 1891. It had previously attracted night life of an unseemly character. With the arrival of the classy Australia, Sydney's bohemian community of artists, writers and musicians yarned in the tea shops set among little stores offering books, pottery and pictures. Some actually lived there. Sydney's first 'little theatre', the Playbox, was established here in 1922.

In winter the popularity of the street diminished as the city winds blew through and sunlight failed to reach it. As Phillip Geeves quoted in *Cazneaux's Sydney 1904 - 1934* it was known as 'Pleurisy Alley'.

Rowe Street photographed by Harold Cazneaux shortly before World War I.

Dymock's Book Arcade

*I*nto the world of Victorian book selling came a bright young man in a white waistcoat, a product of Redfern's Cleveland Street public school: his name was William Dymock. Like other legendary Sydney booksellers, Will Dymock had his apprenticeship behind the counter of the Sydney branch of George Robertson's bookshop. Recognising his capabilities, the firm sent Dymock to London to purchase Australiana but he had other plans and acquired the Australian agency for several British publishers.

Dymock was 21 in 1881 when he opened his bookshop in an upstairs room in Pitt Street. He canvassed and delivered books personally, specialising in collectors' volumes and numbering David Mitchell, of Mitchell Library fame, among his customers.

In December 1890 Dymocks occupied an area below the Royal Hotel in George Street, site of Barney Levey's theatrical venture, calling itself 'the largest Bookshop in the World'. That year Dymock offered Sir Henry Parkes a £2000 advance to write his autobiography.

In 1898 Will Dymock became an Alderman in the Sydney Municipal Council and his prospects seemed brighter than ever when, at the age of 39, he died suddenly of a cerebral haemorrhage at his home at Potts Point.

Dymock never married so his sister, Marjory Forsyth, ran the business. In 1922 the firm bought the site. The old Royal Hotel was demolished and Dymock's Block was completed in 1930. A long established tenant was the June Dally-Watkins Model School and Agency.

In 1974 Dymock's bookshop received a facelift, reaffirming its position as one of the city's major bookshops.

The Royal Hotel in the 1880s. It opened in 1829 in George Street. Sydney's first theatre, the Theatre Royal, was originally located in the back of the first Royal Hotel. The shop on the right, below the veranda, was later occupied by Dymock's bookshop. This building was demolished in 1914 to make way for Dymocks Arcade (ANU Archives of Business and Labour)

When Angus Met Robertson

*I*f publishing is (or was) a 'gentleman's profession' then book selling is truly the 'gentle profession'. The most gentle of men was David Angus who opened a tiny bookshop in Market Street in June 1884 and lent his name to the oldest surviving booksellers in Sydney.

The city's early bookshop history had a strong Scottish accent. Angus and Robertson were Scots and even William Dymock's parents were Scottish although he was born in Chippendale. There were two George Robertsons in the book trade. They not only shared the same name and the same heritage they were both the sons of ministers, both wore beards and both died in their 73rd year. They never met, probably because one George Robertson sold books in Sydney and the other did the same in Melbourne.

The Melbourne Robertson, senior of the two, opened a Sydney branch in George Street, one shop north of King Street. One day in 1882 a 21-year-old Scot who had arrived from New Zealand on the previous day, entered the shop looking for a job. His bookselling experience was good but when he said his name was George Robertson the manager shook his head but he got the job and worked alongside David Angus.

Angus was 29 when he left GR's to open his ten by 20 feet bookshop in Market Street which, according to Banjo Paterson, 'resembled one of those cubicles in any eastern bazaar'. It was here a latter-day Sydney bookseller, Jim Tyrrell, obtained his first job at the age of 12.

David Angus was a consumptive and realising he needed a partner who would take a personal interest he invited black-bearded George Robertson to join him. Robertson paid £15 for his share. In 1890, the start of that rich decade in Australian literature, Angus and Robertson moved into 89 Castlereagh Street, formerly O'Brien's coach building works. The bookshop remained at 89 for the next 81 years.

According to James Tyrrell's autobiography, *Old Books, Old Friends, Old Sydney*, the two partners, although exact opposites, were ideally suited, both men sharing a Scottish heritage and a profound love of books.

When the partners began publishing books half way through the 'nineties, David Angus was full of doubt. It was Robertson, according to Tyrrell, who possessed 'the physique and the energy to make light of a publisher's burdens, enough of the visionary in him to see success ahead and enough of the dictator to stride over obstacles or opposition'.

In April 1895 Banjo Paterson asked Angus and Robertson whether they would publish a collection of his poems. Robertson took the gamble and The Man from Snowy River appeared in print. Its immediate success encouraged Henry Lawson to hand over his manuscript of In the Days When the World Was Wide followed by When the Billy Boils. Their success was evidence that Australians wanted to read more about their country. The huge sales of C.J. Dennis's The Songs of a Sentimental Bloke proved the point.

In 1896 the partners launched the Sydney Book Club Library, the uniformly red-covered titles available for an annual membership of two guineas. Most club members were from rural areas. The book club ceased operating in 1958, two years after the advent of television.

Sadly David Angus was unable to share in the firm's success for long. Illness forced his retirement at the end of 1900 and he returned to Britain for a visit but the damp weather proved too much and he died in Bournemouth in February 1901.

In 1907 Angus and Robertson became a public

Angus and Robertson

company. During the 1920s the company published Norman Lindsay and such ambitious works as C.E.W. Bean's *Official History of Australia in the War of 1914-18* and the handsome two volume green bound *Australian Encyclopedia*.

The company also acquired a printery calling it Halstead Press, after George Robertson's birthplace. When 'G.R.', as he was fondly called, died in 1933 his obituary acclaimed him as 'the best friend Australian literature ever had'. The loss of this dour but kind and generous man was deeply felt in the literary world.

The company expanded rapidly after 1960 with a bewildering exchange of shares and ownership. The company lost something of its literary personality when it lost a number of its long-time employees in the early 1970s. In recent years the name has been franchised to booksellers around the country and the company has established overseas interests.

In 1986 Angus and Robertson celebrated its hundredth birthday. No doubt the ghosts of the founders were present, scratching their heads in wonderment but grateful their names have continued to influence Sydney's book world.

Old books, old friends, old Sydney: Tyrrell's Bookshop shoulder to shoulder with Angus and Robertson in Castlereagh Street in December 1925.
(City of Sydney Archives)

Lola's Way

The colonists were flattered and fearful in 1855 at the arrival of celebrated femme fatale, Lola Montez. Everyone knew of her affair with King Ludwig of Bavaria and her dalliance with composer Franz Liszt. Europe's richest men had fallen at her feet but now, at 37, that was all in the past and she took to the stage to enact a romanticised portrayal of her colourful life. It included her notorious Spider Dance attired 'in a minimum of cover for her shapely body while she danced with fiery passion and sensuous movement'.

Arriving in Sydney from San Francisco with her own company she opened at the Royal Victoria in Pitt Street in August 1855. The show sold out for the entire six-week season.

Lola's leading man, Charles Follar, who was also her lover, was so jealous over her enormous popularity he tried to commit suicide by leaping into Darling Harbour. Lola had become bored with Follar and decided she could not only get by without him but also with half the company. She departed for Melbourne on the paddle steamer *Waratah* with the remainder of the company leaving infuriated cast members stranded whereupon they took out a £2000 writ against her for breach of contract.

Bailiff Thomas Brown, raced down to Circular Quay in a hansom cab in time to see the *Waratah* steaming down the Harbour. Undeterred he leapt into a launch in hot pursuit. Lola was enjoying a drink with the ship's captain when Brown burst in waving the writ: either she paid the money immediately or she must accompany him back to Sydney. Lola seemed resigned to returning and excused herself while she went to collect her baggage. Once inside the cabin she locked the door. The bailiff banged and threatened when suddenly the door opened and Lola stood there completely naked.

Brown appealed to the ship's captain who showed little sympathy. The pilot launch was about to return to the Quay, and unless Mr Brown boarded it he would have to go to Melbourne. Faced with the embarrassment of escorting the naked lady, he entered the boat alone. The cast managed to raise their fare back to America, Charles Follar killed himself and Lola Montez went on to shock the good citizens of Melbourne.

Lola Montez who shocked Sydney with her 'Spider Dance' at the Royal Victoria Theatre in Pitt Street in 1855.

The Longest Reign

The old Theatre Royal was demolished in the name of progress in 1972 ending more than a century of theatre-going on the site in Castlereagh Street, around the corner from King Street.

The first curtain rose in March 1855 when Joseph Wyatt, a former Pitt Street haberdasher, opened his Prince of Wales Theatre on the site. The rush for gold created a shortage of tradesmen and costs mounted to a ruinous £30 000. Although larger and better equipped than its rival, the Royal Victoria, audiences weren't big enough to maintain two theatres of that size and after three years Wyatt was forced to sell at one third of what he paid for it. In 1860 Wyatt, who once owned property all over Sydney, died an impoverished and disillusioned man. That year a fire started in the adjoining bakery and spread to the roof of the theatre which ended a blackened waste. The title of the play at the time was *A Very Serious Affair*.

The site was bought by R. Fitzgerald who offered a prize for the best theatre design. In May 1863 the Prince of Wales reopened in the presence of the Governor and his wife, Sir John and Lady Young. Although the first fully mechanical theatre in Australia it failed to impress audiences even though honoured by presence of the Duke of Edinburgh in 1868.

The theatre kept going until it was razed by the biggest conflagration seen in Sydney to that time. A shameful altercation occurred between rival volunteer fire fighting companies who fought over the possession of a handy water plug. They forgot their differences when three firemen were killed by a collapsing wall. The theatre reopened December 1875 as the Theatre Royal.

In 1874 the American couple, J.C. Williamson and his wife, Maggie Moore, arrived in Australia to appear in their successful play *Struck Oil*. They returned five years later with the rights to *HMS Pinafore* acquired from W.S. Gilbert for £300. It was a spectacular success and the couple decided to stay and form the J.C. Williamson Company.

'The Firm', as it was nicknamed, brought out Sarah Bernhardt in 1891 to appear in *Camille* at Her Majesty's where she was the toast of the town. Williamson became sole proprietor of the company that year when his marriage broke up: he went off with a dancer and his wife eloped with an actor.

Theatres were lit with oil or gas and the proximity of naked flame to painted canvas resulted in frequent theatre fires. On 16 June 1892 the Theatre Royal went up in smoke, although the outcome was less drastic than on previous occasions, parts of the stage and ceiling were damaged. 'The Firm' took over the Royal and had it remodelled in 1921. J.C. died eight years earlier while visiting Paris.

'The Firm' held a monopoly over the Australian stage well into the twentieth century and reluctant to take risks imported overseas successes which are said to have impeded the progress of local productions. In 1972 the Theatre Royal was demolished to make way for the MLC Centre and a new Theatre Royal reopened as part of the complex.

Looking east from Pitt Street in the late 1880s. Quong Tart's Tea Rooms are on the right; the Theatre Royal on the left. (Henry King)

Wild About Harry

Harry Rickards, 26, dressed as a top-hatted 'toff' and twirling a cane swaggered on to the Sydney stage in 1871 and had audiences in stitches with his upper-class monologues and cockney ditties. It was Harry who established an Australian vaudeville tradition when he leased the Garrick Theatre in Castlereagh Street in 1893. The site had music hall associations ever since the Scandinavian Hall was built in 1868 although the 'Old Scan' was more of a grog shop where entertainment came free with the booze. The Hall burned down and a proper theatre went up in its place. It was called the Garrick, not after the 18th century London actor, after a local baker!

Harry, who drifted back and forth between his native London and Sydney decided to settle in the Antipodes. He renamed the theatre the Tivoli where he presented black-faced minstrels in velvet red coats and candy-striped pants jangling tambourines between 'Why did the chicken cross the road' jokes.

Harry introduced the first moving pictures to Australia when he featured an American conjurer who showed his Cinematograph to a 'crammed house' in 1896. This 'startling novelty', said the *Herald*, showed crowds promenading along London's Strand, traffic on Westminster Bridge and a boxing match 'that was hissed'. During one performance a man fell from the gallery to the stalls, overcome perhaps by the novelty of the moving pictures.

September 1899 saw the inevitable fire. It seemed like the end for Harry who should have taken heart when his lucky horseshoe was saved from the

The Victoria Hall replaced 'Old Scan' in Castlereagh Street, near Market Street. In 1890 it opened as the Garrick Theatre but the stage was too small for drama so in 1893 entrepreneur Harry Rickards turned it into the first Tivoli vaudeville theatre. The Embassy Cinema replaced the 'Tiv' in 1929. This photo was taken in 1881. (NSW Government Printer)

smouldering ruins. The New Tivoli opened the following year with Harry himself performing one of his Champagne Charlie routines.

Although he objected to 'objectionable vulgarisms' on stage he didn't object when reigning queen of the British music hall, Marie Lloyd, in her cartwheel hat and ostrich feathers sang risque songs and recited saucy verses with wide-eyed innocence. Tivoli audiences loved it.

Local entertainers like Roy 'Mo' Rene, Gus Bluett, Carrie Moore and Gladys Moncrieff became household names thanks to the 'Tiv'.

Harry died in 1911 unaware moving pictures would one day overtake his theatre. J.C Williamson took over the Tiv in 1924 and demolished it four years later replacing it with the Embassy Picture Theatre.

In 1933 J C Williamson acquired the Grand Opera House at the railway end of Castlereagh Street and renamed it the Tivoli. 'Solely for people seeking entertainment by tumblers, magicians and leg shows' sniffed one observer but it appealed to the masses.

By the 1950s 'variety' entertainment was on its way out. In 1970 the Lend Lease Development Corporation which had taken over the site sent in the demolisher and the 60-year-old theatre, with all its memories, disappeared.

Top: The original Tivoli Theatre in Castlereagh Street in Harry Rickard's day.

Bottom: The art deco Embassy in 1934 was designed by Charles Bohringer. It replaced the Tivoli.

'Meet you at The Australia'

When he laid the foundation stone for the Hotel Australia in 1889 the venerable Premier, Sir Henry Parkes, recalled the time when Sydney had 'only one small coffee house which was denoted by a brown loaf, a pumpkin and a pound of uncooked steak in the window'. Parkes had arrived in the colony as a young married immigrant 50 years earlier.

The Hotel Australia, on the west side of Castlereagh Street between Martin Place and King Street, replaced a nest of back alleys and a terrace of cottages once belonging to successful merchant Mary Reiby. The magnificent seven-storey building brought international hotel standards to a city familiar with such colonial hostelries as Pettys, Pulteneys and the Royal. The public took great pride in its elaborate facade and domed tower when the hotel opened 11 July 1891. Merely entering its elegant portico and ascending the marble staircase made one feel superior.

The structure had been threatened by the fire that destroyed an entire block in Martin Place the previous October. Manager Edwin Moore worried whether the flames would reach the unfinished hotel, as jets from the fire hoses weren't powerful enough to reach above the second floor. Fortunately the hotel was out of the reach of the fire but it frightened the owners into installing fireproof iron sheeting between the floors.

The first signature to appear on the hotel register was that of celebrated French actress Sarah Bernhardt who appeared in *Camille* at Her Majesty's in Pitt Street. She was expected on the morning of 11 July but arrived in the afternoon instead. It appears the train at Spencer Street, Melbourne, generously waited for her while a member of her staff galloped in a hansom cab back to the hotel in St. Kilda where she left her pet tortoise. When the train finally puffed into Sydney, barriers were flung aside and 'an excited throng surged in towards the approaching carriages' without stopping to purchase platform tickets.

Mr Moore, lined up in the foyer with his staff to escort her to one of the six hydraulic lifts, must have blinked in amazement when Madame swept in followed by her entourage laden with baggage and a menagerie of pets which included caged birds, a St Bernard dog, a pug, a 'native bear' and the tortoise! Madame graciously announced she had not felt as much at home since leaving Paris.

The Australia's palatial bar was a favourite meeting place for businessmen while generations of women paused at the Australia during their city shopping expeditions to enjoy afternoon tea and cakes to the accompaniment of the Palm Court string quartet.

When British author, Arnold Haskell, visited Sydney during World War II he found 'unlike Melbourne, Sydney has its Cafe Society. The centre of this life is the Hotel Australia, an enormous modern hotel with five restaurants at varying prices'.

The grand old hotel, so long the focal point of Sydney's social life, disappeared in the 1960s and is scarcely known of by a new generation.

The Hotel Australia, Sydney's first international-class hotel, in the early 1890s.
(Royal Australian Historical Society)

The bar at the Australia at 5.30pm in 1953 and not a female customer in sight. The hotel was the centre of Sydney's social life for 75 years.

Cosmopolitan King Street

For generations King Street was the twinkle in Sydney's eye - for of all the city streets, none epitomised the extrovert, carefree side of the city's personality as much as cosmopolitan King Street. Even the massive monoliths now occupying the street have failed to completely smother the street's special charm.

It was named in 1810, three years after Philip Gidley King, third governor of NSW. King had left the colony a sick and defeated man, having failed to suppress the 'scurrility and abuse' of monopolist traders and corrupt military officers.

King Street had three distinct personalities: the top end was legal; the centre lively, the lower end loitered down to the docks. Unlike most city streets, King Street is luminous with people at night thanks to the theatres in the vicinity. 'Sydney's Piccadilly' an over-zealous colonial once called it. Some of the nineteenth century lingers in the ornamental stone facades above some shops but concrete 'centres' have stolen the sunshine and the soul from the street.

King Street is a street of memories, of food shops and dress shops not forgotten, of cafes, clubs and corner taverns and the characters who haunted them. There was the Oxford Hotel on the Phillip Street corner where frowning bewigged gentlemen in billowing black gowns still stride across the road. Twenty-two hotels served drinks the length of the street in 1890.

There was scarce a time when King Street was without a bookshop. William Dymock was at 142 in the late 1880s; Rowlandson's NSW Bookstall opened even earlier at 130. In modern times the Pocket Bookshop moved around from Hosking Place to the spacious basement of 130 and in the 1960s Berkelouw's secondhand books ventured closer to Castlereagh Street from the bottom end.

King Street was always good for a feed. When Thomas Lewis began selling oysters in 1855 he little dreamt he was starting a tradition which would survive more than 100 years. Early last century, shoppers rested their feet over a cuppa and a scone at Quong Tart's tearooms and when the fruit shop that bore Guiseppe De Luca's surname on the same spot for 101 years, closed its doors on 31 July 1987, a nostalgic sigh sounded from a generation who had enjoyed their delicious fruit salads. Not even modern traders are safe as witnessed when G.J. Coles closed its buoyant Pitt Street corner store, after 35 years, in January 1987.

Mrs Anthony Hordern sold straw bonnets from a shop on the corner of Lee's Court just up from Pitt Street over 170 years ago. John Norton's irreverent weekly, *Truth*, first issued from this laneway in 1890.

King Street has strong journalistic associations. The *Australian Star* absorbed by the afternoon *Sun* was at 74. The *Daily Telegraph* hummed at number 139, long before Frank Packer acquired it in 1936, and the New Zealand Press Association was at 135.

In the late 1880s Sydney boasted a dozen advertising agencies, four in King Street: Hutchinsons, Mandelsons, the Federal Advertising Press Agency and the New South Wales Railway Advertising Company. Their descendants, under other names, probably occupy some multi-storey tower.

The street has its remembered sounds: the pieman's bell, the cry of newspaper sellers and voices of flower girls, 'genuine cockney' wrote a visitor in 1892. Few remember the clip-clop of horses heaving their carts or the tramway cable murmuring beneath the roadway. No one at all remembers the crunch of the redcoat guard returning from Hyde Park Barracks to their quarters in George Street.

One of the street's memorable personalities sold pies, fresh-cooked, on a brazier on the south-east corner of Pitt Street in the 1850s. His name was Billy King universally known as The Flying Pieman. Billy was renowned for his feats of strength; in another age he would have qualified for the Guinness Book of Records. He once carried a large dog from Campbelltown to Sydney in nine hours and a goat from Brickfield Hill to Parramatta in seven hours. He also drew a pretty lady in a gig for half-a-mile. The celebrated and eccentric pie man lost his mind and died in a home for the destitute in 1874.

Less than two weeks after Ned Kelly kept his date with the hangman in November 1880, a noisy crowd packed a small hall on the corner of King and Castlereagh Streets. They came to see two members of the Kelly clan: sister Kate and brother Jim mounted on Ned's grey mare Kitty. The pair arrived in Sydney to cash in on their deceased brother's notoriety. Sydney police were most indignant and turfed out the mob and sent the Kellys packing back to Victoria.

Two ladies seated sedately in a cable tram as it glides up King Street. The white-helmeted traffic constable stands aside at the Castlereagh Street corner in 1900. The cable tram ran for 11 years between Erskine Street wharf and Rose Bay from September 1894.

Left and right: The most photographed corner in the city, the corner of King and George Streets. On the left the famous Darrell Lea corner in the 1890s and the same corner 50 years later.

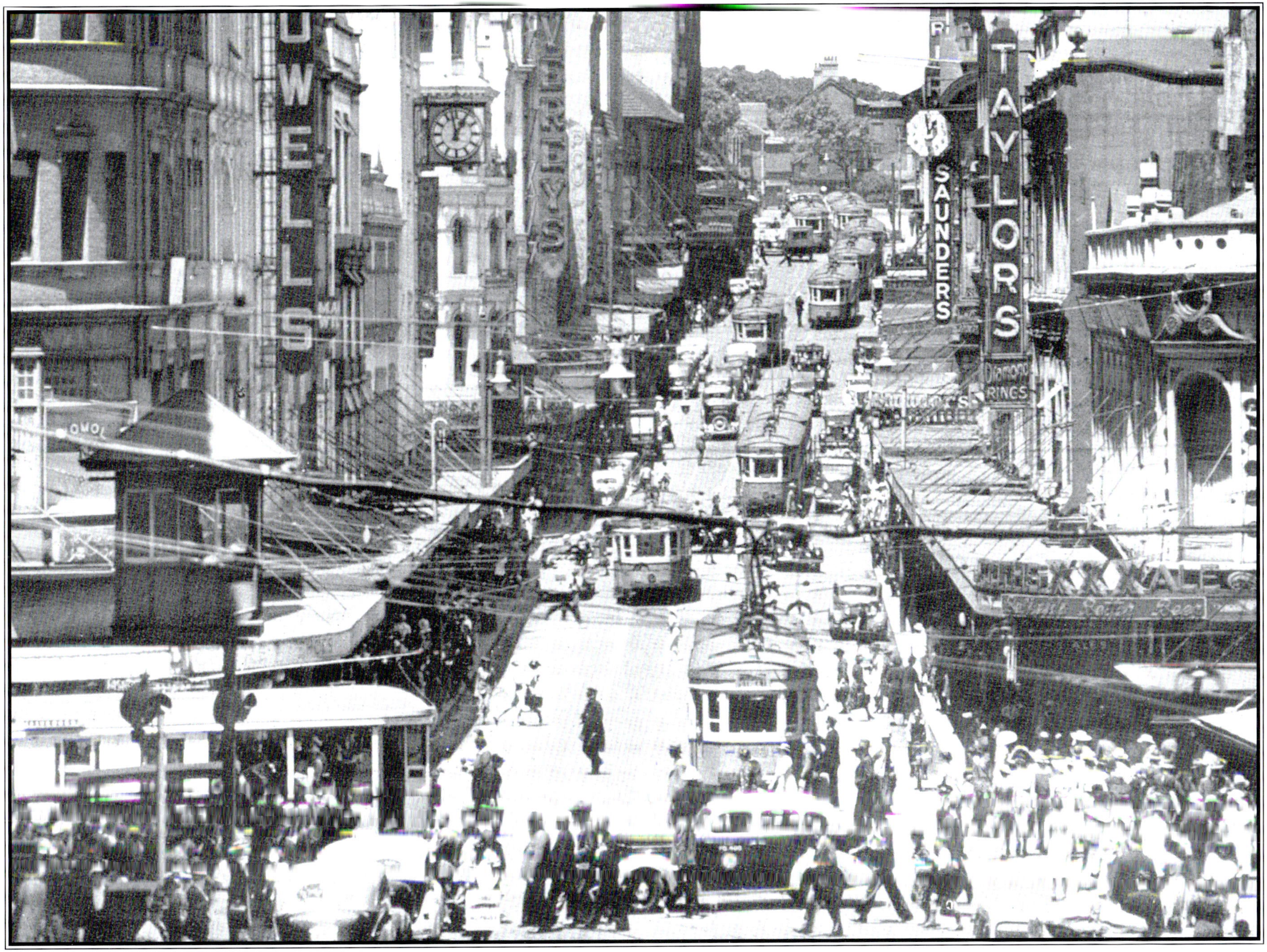
WELLS
VERDEYS
TAYLORS
SAUNDERS
Diamond RINGS
XXX ALE

A view of George Street facing northwards from King Street, with trams still in service. The scene is in the vicinity of Martin Place and the GPO. The clock on the right is attached to the GPO. David Jones is on the corner of Barrack Street with Beard Watsons a few doors down. Beard Watsons sold quality furnishings such as gold framed reproductions and imitation colonial furniture, popular in the 1960s. The Cooee store on the right sold clothing and was situated at 326 George Street. Beside the Cooee was Palings, one of the two great music stores in Sydney, the other being Nicholsons at 416 George Street, the oldest 'Musical Firm' in Sydney. Palings and Co. at 338 George Street sold sheet music, pianos, records, reeds for wind instruments, guitar strings and almost anything any musician could need. Next door to Palings was popular Sargents Refreshment Rooms where the famous Sargents pies and a cup of tea were always available. McDowells was one of the top Sydney stores, a notch down from David Jones. The store had both a King and George Street entrance. McDowells was successful enough to open a store in Dee Why in the 1960s. Palmers, next door to McDowells, were men's outfitters and next door to them was a Fashion Centre for ladies before you turned into King Street. This was one of the busiest sections of George Street.

George Street facing south from Martin Place in May 1961 three months after the last tram departed from Sydney's streets, to return 35 years later under the euphemism 'light rail'. Double-deckers and single decker buses filled the streets with the smell of diesel and the anarchy of the traffic on this stretch of George Street got worse with the departure of trams. This functional part of the city housed Gibb and Beemans, the only optometrist to trust, Kitchings for quality travel goods, Kodak House from which the company operated in Sydney and many other specialist stores. The signage is a trigger to our memory of a time which we only realise has gone when looking at such a photograph. What happened to these established stores?

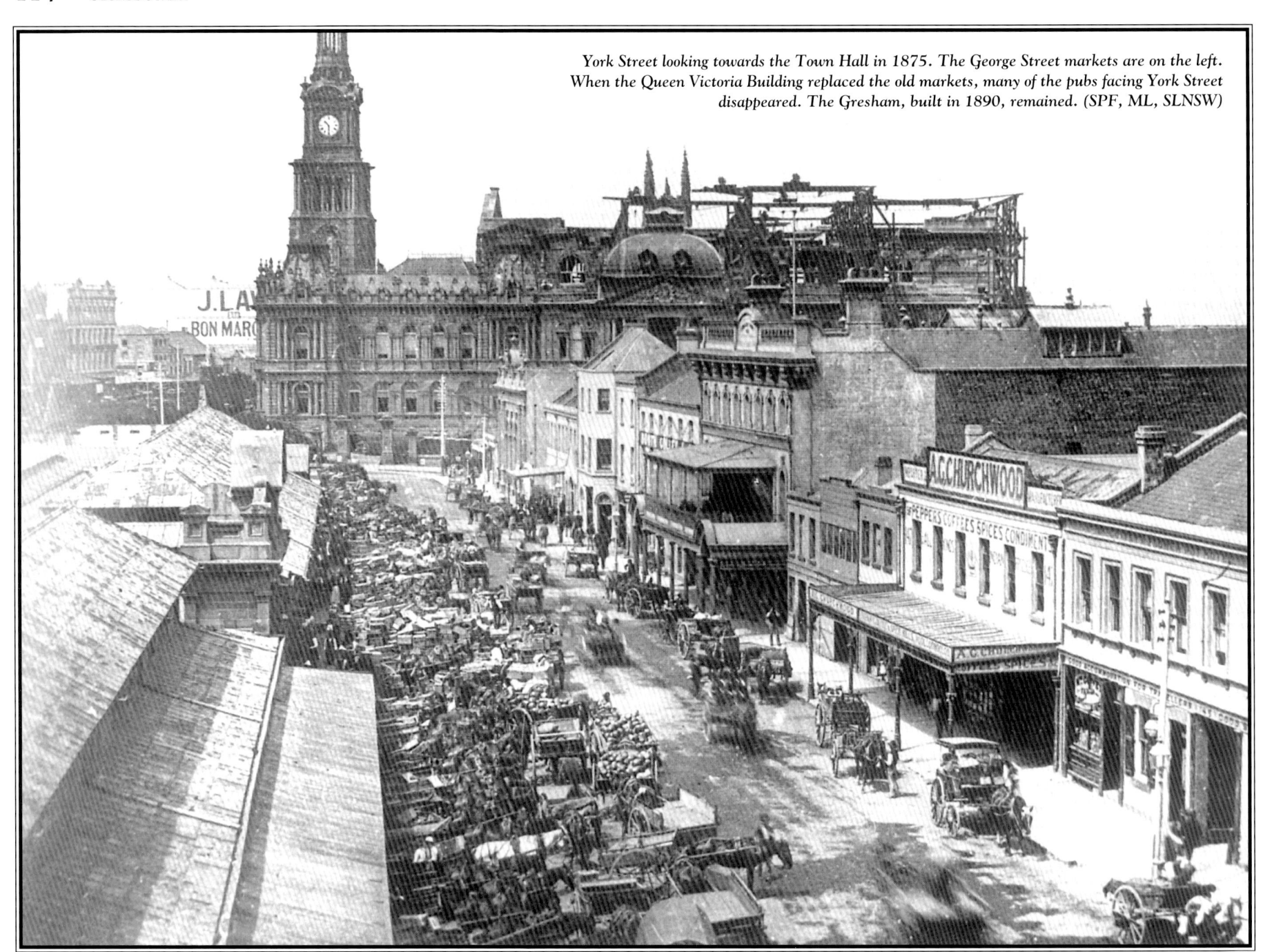

York Street looking towards the Town Hall in 1875. The George Street markets are on the left. When the Queen Victoria Building replaced the old markets, many of the pubs facing York Street disappeared. The Gresham, built in 1890, remained. (SPF, ML, SLNSW)

*The George Street market, predecessor to the Queen Victoria Building, in the 1880s. Saturday night was late shopping night and the boys and girls paraded about, surging onto the car free streets, dodging hansom cabs and trams.
(Tyrrell Collection, National Library of Australia)*

The Old Lady of George Street

The town's first markets were below the present Cahill Expressway. The new site - south along George Street - was chosen by Governor Macquarie where covered in markets were built and a market house, designed by Francis Greenway, faced the burial ground, site of the present Town Hall. Vegetables and fowl were displayed down one side, maize and wheat along the other. Booths down the centre offered drapery and groceries.

An overseas visitor was struck by the butter sellers, young girls 'somewhat sallow and sun-freckled and of majestic stature' with 'sharp chins, wide foreheads, flat faces'. James Maclehose, author of *Stranger's Guide in New South Wales for 1839* likened the structure more to an amphitheatre than a market place and was struck by its cleanliness.

The markets were taken over by the newly-formed Corporation of Sydney in 1846 when beef and mutton sold for twopence a pound, a pound of cheese cost fourpence and a dozen bottles of ale could be bought for 11 shillings.

The taproom was the centre of town gossip. Brown-faced farmers from the west arrived by boat at the wharf at the foot of Market Street or by dray, to yarn with town shopkeepers over a tankard of thick ale while their wives window shopped along George Street.

The market house eventually became a police court and was demolished in 1889. The remainder of the patched and peeling market sheds came down two years later. In 1898 a majestic phoenix arose from the ashes. It was appropriately named the Queen Victoria Building.

The enormous project was undertaken at the height of the economic depression of 1893. Alderman Harris told the crowd the building 'will live with the centuries and stand as a landmark in history' but the Queen Vic turned out to be a white elephant. The building included 30 shops facing George Street and as many fronting York Street with a coffee palace at the Druitt Street end. A modern innovation was a hydraulic lift which lowered horse and carts from York Street to the basement.

Increasing traffic congestion resulted in the markets moving to the Haymarket in 1910 leaving the building to plague one city council after another.

York Street side of the Queen Victoria Building. (SPF, ML, SLNSW))

Changes were made in World War I and continued in an effort to make the Queen Victoria Building economically viable. The interior became a labyrinth of gloomy passages and stairways with a maze of small offices and wine cellars in the basement. The Market Street end was occupied by the cramped and dingy City Library. Library members still recall the wavering cage lift that ascended at a pace in keeping with the horse and buggy era.

In the late 1950s the Queen Victoria Building was costing the council a quarter million pounds a year. There was a tempting suggestion to flatten the Old Lady of George Street and replace it with gardens a block long. Talk of turning it into a gambling casino in the mid-1970s brought a howl of protest from the Church. To the romantic-minded the Queen Vic brought a touch of Arcadia to the city. To antagonists it was an anachronism.

In 1978 extensive damage to the Queen Victoria Building caused by the bomb blast outside the Hilton Hotel opposite, brought the 'massive bulk' back into public focus. The following year tenders were opened for its complete restoration. A Malaysian company won the proposal for a magnificent shopping mall. The $75 million facelift took three years. When the new Queen Victoria Building opened its doors 18 November 1986, there was scarcely a dissenting voice among Sydney's cynical press and public. It had been restored to a level of taste and grandeur inside and out that its original designers would have scarcely thought possible.

The modern cantilevered awning had replaced the Victorian awning around the QVB by the early 1920s.
(City of Sydney Archives)

Sydney's Wedding Cake

The economic depression brought a decline in agricultural prices and the colony's progress to a shuddering halt by 1842. To shift some of the administration's financial burden Governor Gipps told the townspeople to manage their own affairs.

An Act passed 20 July 1842 declared Sydney a city under a mayor and aldermen. The first election was held in November and John Hosking became the first mayor but was forced to resign three months later when his Pitt Street company suffered huge financial losses.

The council met at the Pulteney Hotel opposite the markets in York Street. From here aldermen may have cast a covetous eye on the burial ground but it was years before a decision was made to build on the site. In 1853 a scandal erupted over bribery allegations, rigged elections, neglect and muddle. It was one of four occasions when an entire city council was sacked.

When it was decided to build the Town Hall on the old burial ground, cries of 'desecration' were heard along with rumours that a plague would envelope the city if bodies were disinterred. One wit suggested aldermen were impervious to the plague so it wouldn't matter.

The foundation stone for the new Town Hall was laid by the Duke of Edinburgh, Queen Victoria's second son, 4 April 1868. The original design was by J.H. Wilson but the involvement of other architects is reflected in the building's flamboyant appearance ranging from Italian Renaissance to ponderous Gothic giving an impression of a giant Victorian wedding cake.

A colourful Town Hall personality was 'Honest John' Harris, five times mayor. Irish-born Harris derived his wealth from his kinsman, John Harris, the First Fleet surgeon who lived in Ultimo. In January 1881, robust 'Honest John' sallied forth from the Town Hall, flanked by the Health Officer and Building Inspector, to inspect the city's shocking slums. Invoking the revolutionary City Improvement Act of 1879 he stamped through the hovels around Phillip Street and the Rocks grimacing with disgust and gave the order for 33 hovels to be demolished.

A few weeks later the indomitable Mayor again marched out of the Town Hall trailed by a gaggle of newspapermen who described in detail the tottering walls, the rotting floors and hideous smells that 'cried aloud of sickness and disease'. When Harris was re-elected in 1886 he sacked 250 council employees for 'impairing efficiency'.

The final phase of the Town Hall, the Centennial Hall, was planned for Sydney's hundredth birthday, January 1888, but the opening took place 27 November 1889. Some 7000 citizens behaved with the 'rough good humour and the impudence of irresponsible folk out on a spree' as John Harris, swathed in voluminous purple robes and accompanied by daughter Marion - his wife had recently died - declared the Town Hall open.

The Sydney Town hall has witnessed scenes of physical violence on several occasions. One took place between Alderman Watkins and Alderman Kelly in January 1901. It was over the Mayor's decision to close the bar, which supplied free drinks to aldermen and their visitors, and replaced it with a bookcase. The ensuing fracas invoked the Mayor's remark that the Town Hall was 'the graveyard of reputations'. Time has proved him right.

More carts than cars outside Sydney Town Hall in 1914 showing the now demolished portico. (Public Transport Commission of NSW)

The Trials of St Andrew's

When Governor Macquarie laid the foundation for St Andrew's in 1819, the closest dwelling was a third of a mile away. He had asked Francis Greenway to design a cathedral alongside the town cemetery but investigating Commissioner John Bigge saw no need for a cathedral and recommended the courthouse across from Hyde Park Barracks be redesigned as St James' Church.

Governor Bourke reset Macquarie's foundation stone in 1837 but work slowed as funds dried up. Progress was spasmodic as the economic depression took its bite, construction coming to a halt in 1842 with only the walls in place.

The roofless cathedral was a depressing sight when Edmund Blacket, designer of many Sydney churches, was appointed architect. Again building was held up as workers everywhere downed tools and rushed off to the gold fields.

In 1857, 600 people gathered within the unfinished cathedral to demand its completion. In 1868 Australia's royal visitor, the Duke of Edinburgh, survived an assassination attempt at Clontarf and the public was invited to contribute to the Cathedral Building Fund in gratitude for his recovery. St Andrew's Day, 30 November 1868, was chosen for the grand opening, 50 years after Governor Macquarie laid his foundation stone.

The Japanese invasion scare in 1942 saw the stained-glass windows removed to the Springwood rectory in the Blue Mountains.

Among the Cathedral's memorials is a flag taken from Changi, the Japanese prison camp. A magnificent bible belonging to King Henry VIII, with original doeskin binding, was presented to the Cathedral by the Queen during her first visit to Australia in 1954.

St Andrew's Cathedral. (John Fairfax and Sons)

A Palace for the people

City cinemas designed in the 1920s reflected the personalities of the heads of the two major film exhibitors. Stuart Doyle of Greater Union. Theatres, chose the exuberant 'atmospheric' model; a cautious Frank Thring of Hoyts preferred Gothic temples. The Regent was more of a temple when a cinema bearing the name was built in each of the four eastern capitals.

J.C. Williamson's bought the site in George Street, just down from Bathurst Street, and architect Cedric Ballantyre designed the ornate ceilings and decorated archways with the generous use of marble. Hoyts took the lease and 2000 seats sold out for the opening, 9 March 1928, featuring Greta Garbo and John Gilbert in *Flesh and the Devil*. In those years the manager received patrons while attired in white tie and tails.

Unlike suburban cinemas that tumbled like ninepins before the onslaught of television, most city cinemas stood firm. In 1934 there were 22 city cinemas and 115 in the suburbs. Forty years later the numbers were almost even: 37 in the city, 39 in the suburbs.

When Hoyts' lease expired in 1972, J.C. Williamson sold the theatre to the Fink Family for $5 million. Company director, Leo Fink, spent a half-million turning it into a lyric theatre.

Two highly successful productions were *No No Nanette* and *The Pirates of Penzance*. The NSW Heritage Council tried to place a permanent conservation order on the theatre describing it as 'one of the few surviving cinemas in the picture palace/temple genre'. The owners objected claiming four times the amount already spent was needed to upgrade the Regent.

In the mid-1980s survival depended on a tug of war between the Regent and the Capitol Theatre: one to be sacrificed for the survival of the other. Historically, the Capitol was favoured because its exterior dated back to 1892. Architects, builder's labourers and the general public all had their say but nothing could save the regal Regent.

Patrons queue outside the Regent in 1937 to see Lloyds of London. *(Home and Away, ML, SLNSW)*

'You're the Cream in my Coffee'

It was the era of big bands in bow ties, of sleek female vocalists, Crosby-style crooners and ballroom dancing. Everyone was mad about movies which brought light into the dark Depression years out of which the nation was slowly emerging in 1936. Now Sydneysiders were to find glamour on their doorstep with the gala opening on 3 April of the Trocadero, next to the Regent, in George Street.

The 'Troc' lived up to its promise with popular Frank Coughlan conducting the band and floor space for 2000 with scores of pretty waitresses. Frank was happy to play requests and the first to be called for was 'You're The Cream in my Coffee'. In those days couples arrived together or arranged to meet in the foyer. Things changed during the war when the Trocadero became a mecca for (white only) American servicemen and local girls. A wartime highlight was the arrival of Artie Shaw and his US Navy Band in 1944 when thousands had to be turned away.

Companies held annual balls there and the Black and White Ball was a social event. In 1954 the ballroom was decorated for the reception of the young Queen. Television and rock and roll saw the decline of ballroom dancing and of the Trocadero. Frank Coughlan's band was still playing on the last night, 5 February 1971, when the same man who requested 'You're The Cream in my Coffee' 35 years earlier, asked for it to be played again.

Frank Coughlan's daughter, Joan Ford, who wrote 'Meet Me at the Trocadero' arranged to put her father's dance band music on CD and cassette, in 1998 and it is available for the adventurous seeker of recorded music.

A flashpowder photograph of a large group of women in front of the bandstand celebrating a 2CH Christmas party on the 15 December 1937. The famous bandstand is in the background. The Trocadero was a popular venue for company functions. The photographer was Sam Hood. (Home and Away, ML, SLNSW)

The Hordern Dynasty

The name Hordern was first heard in Sydney in 1825 when Anthony and Anne Hordern, a couple in their thirties, arrived with their three children as free passengers in the convict ship *Phoenix*.

Anthony was a coach builder and opened a coach workshop in King Street, down from Castlereagh Street. Anne opened a haberdashery next door. In 1834 she advertised 'Bargains in Bonnets' and 'Ladies stays boned to order.'

Eldest son, Anthony the Second, was 20 when he visited Melbourne where land was offered at a pittance. He was so impressed he persuaded his parents to move to Melbourne where they bought three town lots and opened a drapery store.

In Sydney young Hordern opened a drapery store with his brother in George Street, their trademark being an oak tree with the motto 'While I Live I'll Grow.' The partnership ended ten years later and Anthony the Second opened a store in the Haymarket bringing his two sons into the business and changing the name to Anthony Hordern and Sons. As the business flourished the store expanded into adjacent premises, the range of goods justifying the claim of 'Universal Providers'. When Anthony the Third died brother Sam became sole proprietor employing, at its peak, 3,500 and operating a fleet of 200 carts. In the 1890s there were six city outlets bearing the Hordern name.

In 1901 a devastating fire destroyed the Haymarket complex. Sam Hordern bought up eighty properties in the block bounded by George, Goulburn and Pitt Streets and in September 1905 opened the giant Palace Emporium.

Sam died four years later and son, Sam the Second, took over. In 1926 he sold the company to private investors for £3 million realising, with an eye on the new city railway and the forthcoming Harbour Bridge, that southern George Street would lose its prominence leaving the Palace Emporium 'like a stranded whale'. The real decline began in the 1950s when a new generation found the store old-fashioned. In October 1969 the grand old store closed its doors for the last time. Make-shift offices occupied some of the floors and temporary shops moved in at street level. In 1981 the building was sold to Malaysian-Chinese property developers. The city's tallest apartment building now occupies the site of what was once the biggest department store building in the southern hemisphere.

The 'universal providers' Anthony Hordern and Sons on the corners of George, Goulburn and Pitt Streets.

The Haymarket Fire

On Wednesday morning, 10 July 1901, Sydney witnessed one of the most spectacular fires in its history. It began at 8.20 am when hundreds of staff were already at their work places and early shoppers wandered through the five buildings, bound by George, Gipps (now Barlow) and Pitt Streets, which made up Anthony Hordern & Sons department store.

It began in the basement toy department of the Palace Building, the centre of the complex, when a fuse wire ignited the celluloid toys and spread rapidly to other inflammable items. Water buckets were useless and the fire roared to the ground floor turning the haberdashery department into a blazing inferno. Employees ran through the building screaming to those on the upper floors to get out as horse-drawn fire engine bells drew closer.

Realising the Palace Building was lost, firemen turned their attention to other buildings in the complex. A strong westerly was blowing and tongues of flame leapt across the narrow lanes separating the blocks.

In the basement of the adjacent furniture building the store engineer and his assistant turned on the engine to pump water to hoses on the upper floors. On the fifth floor of the eight-storey block three staff members manned the hoses directing the jets across Parker Street to the Palace Building. In the street below, Harry Clegg, 22, from upholstery, watched the fruitless efforts of the men on the fifth floor and deciding they needed help dashed inside and bounded up the stairs.

The four men now directing the hoses were unaware the lower floors of their own building were already ignited; someone had to warn them. Furniture storeman Bill Farrell and the Deputy Fire Superintendent coughed and spluttered their way through the smoke to the fifth floor with flames following them up the stairs. Two of the men made a dash down through the flames and staggered into the street badly burned. Farrell and a second man, John Nicholl, chose instead to make for the goods lift on the fourth floor. The two men slithered down the steel cable and Farrell; the slighter of the two, wriggled through the trapdoor while Nicholl remained on the roof of the lift which made the slow descent through the roaring flames. Farrell collapsed when he got out into the fresh air. Nicholl burned to death.

The two men pumping water from the basement were momentarily forgotten but they were already incinerated. The death toll stood at three but two men remained on the fifth floor: furniture storeman Bob Malcolm and Harry Clegg. While others risked the stairway and lift, Clegg and Malcolm panicked and raced upstairs to escape the flames. The pair reached the roof with the fire climbing inexorably up towards them. Their last refuge was a brick parapet overlooking the street. Malcolm slipped backwards into the flames, Clegg climbed up and managed to support himself. From the street a huge crowd watched the drama unfolding high above them.

The extended fire ladder was 40 feet short of the lone figure clinging to the parapet. Women were crying and men growled with frustration. The flames were all around Harry Clegg and the crowd below gasped in horror as they saw his jacket catch alight. He tore off the jacket and suddenly flung his cap into the air. He appeared to crouch in prayer for a few moments and screams rose from the throng below as they saw him dive to his death.

By early afternoon Sydney's largest department store was a black, smouldering ruin. Five buildings were destroyed and five men were dead. The store operated from Sydney Showground until the grand emporium on Brickfield Hill was completed. Anthony Hordern's was to last another 60 years.

Thousands hurried to the Haymarket to witness the spectacular Anthony Hordern's fire when five men died in 1901. (Evening News)

The Theatre Under the Stars

To relax in an exotic Florentine garden while enjoying movies under the stars was the grand illusion of Stuart Doyle, flamboyant managing director of Greater Union Theatres. When the Capitol Theatre opened in the Haymarket in June 1928 the public were entranced by the 'atmospheric' theatre's starry firmament ceiling, its 'garden walls' and Grecian columns. Stuart Doyle had a talent for making news, had he lived in the US he may have been another Goldwyn or Mayer.

Doyle came in on the ground floor of the Australian film industry in 1910 and formed Greater Union Theatres which merged several film exhibiting circuits. In 1921, when movie audiences were multiplying, the company began remodelling many of the barn-like movie houses that mushroomed in the last decade. The Capitol, the first of his 'million dollar theatres', was followed by the State Theatre in Market Street and the State in Melbourne.

The Haymarket building first housed the Belmore Markets and in 1914 the Sydney Council redesigned the interior for Wirth's Circus naming it the Hippodrome. It soon became apparent the council had another 'white elephant' on its hands. When Greater Union Theatres offered to turn it into cinema the council was delighted but the directors of Greater Union were not; they were convinced the movie-going public would avoid Campbell Street in the heart of Sydney's seedy Chinatown. Doyle's forceful personality won the day and he engaged Sydney theatre architect, Henry White, who based his design on the new 'atmospheric' theatres springing up in America.

The exterior walls of the former markets were left standing and the interior was entirely rebuilt. The program featured an orchestra which ascended on an hydraulic platform and a Wurlitzer organ which wheezed popular melodies. Variety acts added to the entertainment for the crowds that came to Campbell Street.

The Depression meant fewer could afford much needed escapism and the company fell on hard times. Doyle was persuaded to resign in 1937 for, like many successful entrepreneurs, he took too many risks. He died in 1945 when Australia's movie-going audience was at its peak. The Capitol, like most movie houses, went into decline when television arrived in 1956. Fortunately for Greater Union Theatres the lease on the Capitol expired in the 1960s and the theatre was plunged into darkness. The aging theatre received a new lease of life when Her Majesty's Theatre burned down and the remainder of the opera season was transferred to the Capitol. The spectacular success of the last show, *Jesus Christ Superstar* at the Capitol in the 1970s, brought back memories of the theatre's heyday.

The doors of the Capitol finally closed in the early 1980s and its darkened interior became the refuge of a colony of cats. When talk of demolition arose, an active lobby of architects, moviegoers and urban historians put up a strong case for its survival and the NSW Heritage Council placed a two-year conservation order on it. In August 1987 the City Council put the matter before the public and the theatre was thrown open to any who wished to inspect the building and pass judgment on its preservation. The verdict was unanimous: the Capitol Theatre must be saved … and it was.

The Capitol Theatre stands on this site today. Pictured here is the Belmore Markets which stood next door to the old Paddy's Market between Hay and Campbell Streets. The new Haymarket was built between 1908 and 1914, conveniently located near Darling Harbour and the railway. On 7 June 1928 the Capitol Theatre opened. Photographed in the 1890s by Charles Kerry. (Tyrrell Collection, National Library of Australia)

Chinatown

Among the various nationalities who descended on Australia in the gold rush years of the 1850s were large numbers of Chinese. Many stayed on when it was all over. They usually settled in their own communities, working as labourers or opening small businesses in locations that came to be known as Chinatown. Others became market gardeners on the city's fringe, while later low cost Chinese restaurants appeared in the suburbs.

In 1861 there were some 13 000 Chinese living in New South Wales, the main location in Sydney being Lower George Street below The Rocks. When the fruit and vegetable market moved from what became the site of the Queen Victoria to the Belmore Markets, the Haymarket and Surry Hills areas became the focus for Sydney's Chinese citizens.

When anti-immigration legislation was passed in 1888 a Royal Commission into 'Alleged Chinese Gambling and Immorality' opened three years later. Opium 'dens' and gambling 'dens' and prostitution were in evidence but the large percentage of Chinese went about their business peaceably and morally.

The Commission failed to stop the antipathy directed towards the Chinese community at the time, especially by the larrikin element but it was dying down by the time of Federation and finally disappeared during World War I.

Campbell Street in 1890: Chinese people worked in Campbell, Sussex and Dixon Streets (known as Chinatown), around the Haymarket area. Traders like Wing Sang and Co. imported goods which were shipped to Darling Harbour and he later exported Australian fruit to China. He opened a new store on the corner of Sussex and Hay Streets, closer to the new markets. (City of Sydney Archives)

Paddy's Market

With fruit and vegetables coming into the city, the closure of the George Street markets and the inadequacy of Belmore and Paddy's markets, the new Haymarket (today's Paddy's Markets) was built. It offered access through many doors so carts and trucks could move freely in and out. The congestion in Campbell street and the overpowering fumes from horse manure and urine forced the Council to purchase a site close to the new Central Railway and the light rail and shipping facilities of Darling Harbour. One early site chosen, demolished and then scrapped was Wexford Street where the Chinese community lived. Wentworth Avenue covers the old Wexford Street area.

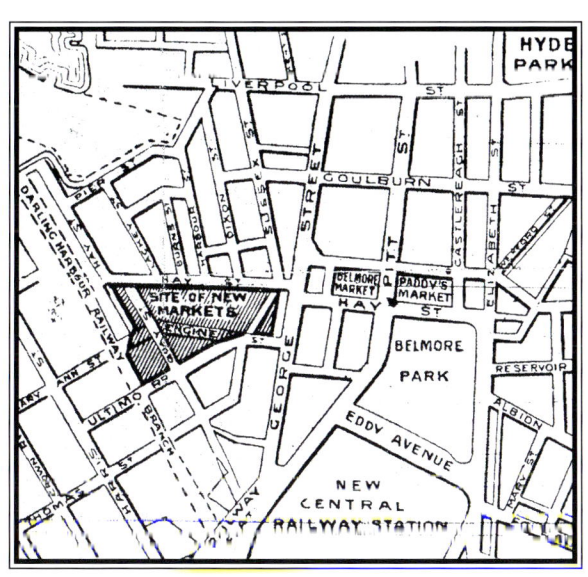

The Haymarket in the 1930s operated as Paddy's Market until 1988. For five years business was relocated to Eveleigh Street railway workshops until the markets returned to this refurbished site. (Sunshine Produce)

A plan of the new markets in 1908. (News Limited)

Campbell Street from Castlereagh Street, looking towards George Street in 1909. The original Paddy's Market is on the left and the Belmore Market, on the corner of Pitt Street, is beside it.

Darling Harbour: Wasteland to Wonderland

Once it was a place of broad tidal flats where the silence was broken by the plop of a fish, a signal to the solitary native, spear poised, moving swiftly through the dense mangroves. The Aborigines were to share the inlet west of Sydney Cove with the first white men who came to snare mud crabs and dig for cockles (giving rise to the name Cockle Bay). It remained undisturbed until Governor Macquarie saw the advantages of its location and with unlimited convict labour at call reclaimed land along the eastern foreshore in order to lay roads and build wharves.

By the time Governor Ralph Darling bestowed his unloved name on the basin several years after Macquarie's departure, it became the tradesmen's entrance for coastal shipping. The industrialisation of Darling Harbour was underway in the 1840s with the steady reclamation of the foreshore. Together with Ultimo and the once pristine Pyrmont peninsular this was to become the city's industrial heartland. Terraces of tight little cottages housing families of dockside employees mushroomed in the vicinity which soon deteriorated into the city's worst slums. The fall of the tide on summer days in the 1870s gave rise to an intolerable stench from the sewage outfall at Darling Harbour and Blackwattle Bay. Railway goods yards and sombre wool warehouses were to complete the bleak Darling Harbour landscape. Out of sight, out of mind was a common attitude of Victorian Sydney and the public gaze was fixed on Hyde Park and the glorious harbour.

The inauguration of the container system gave road transport precedence over rail, marking the decline of the gaunt vista of blackened brick and rusting metal. It also began the protracted controversy, almost equalling that over the Opera House, on the future of the site.

Where goods trains shunted in the shadow of massive warehouses by the late 1980s a huge concourse was created - flanked by conference and entertainment centres, multiple restaurants, an aquarium, a Chinese garden and the ambitious Maritime Museum. Development of the area continues apace establishing Darling Harbour as Sydney's official entertainment centre.

The first Pyrmont Bridge opened in 1857 and was demolished 30 years later. The present bridge opened in 1902. The bridge gave Ryde fruit growers easier access to the George Street markets where the Queen Victoria Building is today. (SPF, ML, SLNSW)

Darling Harbour needed coal to fuel the steam locomotives which shuttled goods from ships to rail yards at Central. (John Buckland Collection, National Library of Australia)

Sussex Street: the Back Door

If George Street was Sydney's shop front, Sussex Street was the tradesmen's entrance. Named by Governor Macquarie in 1810, the street was hewn out of rock bordering Darling Harbour. In 1836 a single wharf at the northern end competed with jetties at Circular Quay. Tiny cottages sprouted and were occupied by people with quaint occupations: boot closer, chandler, and a teacher of the quadrille. A slaughter yard was established out of sight at the foot of Druitt Street in the 1840s, setting the tone for dirty, dusty, industrious Sussex Street.

The face of Sussex Street changed as it ran from south to north. At the southern end mud flats gave way to narrow streets. Stone warehouses cast their shadow further along the street.

Lodging houses, cafes and one-storey terraces shouldered along Sussex Street north of Erskine Street. World War I Prime Minister Billy Hughes would one day live here. It was all cleared away in the 1880s when mammoth warehouses were built to service the new wharves in Day Street created from reclaimed land.

The hub of Sussex Street lay between Market and King Street with rows of little shops shaded by overhead verandas lined both sides of the street. A pub on almost every corner made sure no one went thirsty in Sussex Street, some sites have accommodated a hotel for over a century.

A vacant block stood diagonally opposite the Sir Walter Scott Hotel on the Sussex-Bathurst Street corner in 1866. One morning an 11-year-old boy was playing on the site with his dog who began scratching among a pile of rubble and turned up a human skull. It led to the arrest of a butcher's assistant named William Henry Scott.

Scott had murdered and dissected his wife. Most of her remains were deposited in the cesspit at the rear of the Sir Walter Scott. The lady's head must have been an afterthought. Scott went to the gallows protesting his innocence in spite of the weight of evidence

The first Pyrmont Bridge opened in 1857, linking outlying Balmain by road and giving Sussex Street a boost. When it was demolished 30 years later it kept local householders in firewood for years. The present bridge opened in 1902.

After the 1950s Sussex Street slowly lost its importance. Pubs such as The Royal George, the Bristol Arms, known as 'The Bunch', and the boisterous Big House in Day Street hung on. Office workers from neighbouring commercial blocks crowd the bars on Friday nights. Today the trend to convert the remaining warehouses into multiple flats is seeing a return to residential living in Sussex Street just as it was a century or more ago.

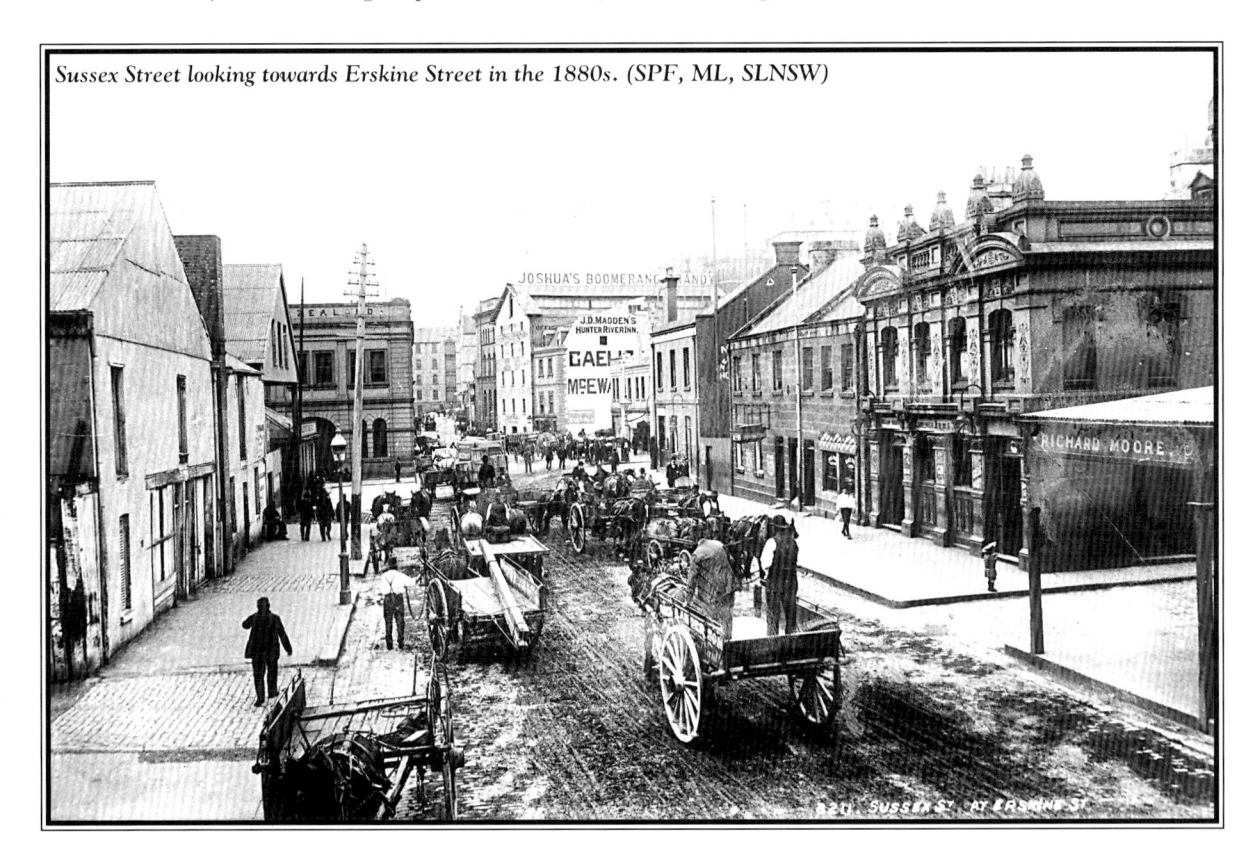

Sussex Street looking towards Erskine Street in the 1880s. (SPF, ML, SLNSW)

The Hungry Mile

Wharf labourers were among the worst affected by the Depression of the 1930s, when the flood of work on the waterfront reduced to a trickle. Dozens of ships lay idle and cargo was barely sufficient to fill half the ships still operating. The wharfies tramped the 'Hungry Mile', the stretch of wharves from Walsh Bay to Pyrmont Bridge. 'These Sussex Street men seeking work outside the wharf gates could only be compared to a flock of birds swarming around to pick up crumbs,' recalled Captain James Gaby in his memoir *The Restless Waterfront*. 'The foreman would stand at the wharf gate to pick up perhaps forty men from a crowd of between three or four hundred desperate and hungry men ... the keen disappointment of those turned away was pitiful to witness.' Often they 'dossed' around the wharf at night hoping to catch a midnight pick-up. 'Those who missed out drifted off to the pub or sadly caught the tram home.'

When Australia found itself affluent in the post-war years constant industrial demands by striking waterside workers were partly in retaliation for those harsh and hungry years.

Sussex Street in the mid 1890s looking south. McMillan's Hotel can be seen on one corner of Margaret Street, on the left hand side in the middle of the photograph. The striped barber's pole on the opposite corner was a tobacconist store. By then steamships were rapidly replacing sail. (Tyrrell Collection, National Library of Australia)

The Wail of the Train Whistle

The first wail of the train whistle heralded the birth of modern Australian. Virgin bush became fenced farm paddocks; clusters of bark huts grew into townships and the gleaming rails led straight back to the city with the markets and the sailing clippers waiting in Sydney Harbour.

Shops shut, businesses closed and few people stayed at home that day, a public holiday, 26 September 1855. They came by cart and buggy, on horseback or on foot to the Cleveland Paddocks to gape at the colony's first railway train. The morning was wet and cloudy when Governor Sir William Denison arrived just before 11 am.

The train was divided into two first class, four second class and five third class four-wheel carriages. There was a wild scramble for the remaining seats. Driver William Sixsmith gave a shrill blast on the engine whistle, a 21-gun salute boomed from the artillery battery and loud cheers arose from the throng when the first train moved off at 11.20 am on its journey linking Sydney with the second oldest settlement, Parramatta.

The non-stop excursion carried passengers past waving crowds at the four intermediate stations: Newtown, Ashfield, Burwood and Homebush and steamed into Parramatta Station (near the present Granville Station) 40 minutes later. The vice-regal party enjoyed a hearty luncheon at the Woolpack Hotel before returning to Sydney. The following day the *Sydney Morning Herald* wrote:

'Thousands who before were averse to railways, thousands who sneered in their ignorance of the advantages they offered, thousands who were timid as to the capacity and safety of the colonial line - now became staunch friends of the railway enterprise.'

The Sydney rail terminus in 1890, when it was known as Redfern Station. At that time the current Redfern Station was known as Eveleigh Station. When Central Railway Station opened on its present location in 1906, the name of Redfern was transferred. (Public Transport Commission of NSW)

Sydney's Non-Central Station

Sydney's first railway station was a single wooden platform housed inside a corrugated iron shed. A brick enclosure was built in 1873 with additional sheds and workshops. In 1888, Edward Eddy became Chief Commissioner for Railways. Eddy was a gifted Scottish engineer with a forceful personality who set about streamlining the railway's operation. His first concern was for the rail gauge to be standardised throughout the colonies. Everyone recognised the need but it was 70 years before passengers journeyed from one state to another without changing trains at the border.

A few years after the line opened in 1855, a scheme was put forward to extend Sydney's rail terminal into the heart of the city. Successive parliaments debated the question and the inevitable Royal Commission sat but each time the matter was shelved. Besides, the prospect of turning Hyde Park into a railway yard filled people with horror.

In 1899 the Minister for Public Works, Edward O'Sullivan, sketched the layout for a large station on the north side of Devonshire Street but the Commissioners shook their collective heads. Nothing short of an extension right into the heart of the city would meet traffic requirements. They were overruled when Parliament approved the building of a large terminal station north of the old one. It meant the disappearance of certain streets and several historic buildings and the carving up of the old Devonshire Street cemetery. The remains of early pioneers were disinterred and conveyed by steam tram and cart to the cemetery at Bunnerong or were reinterred in inner city cemeteries. The long pedestrian subway between George Street West (Railway Square) and Strawberry Hills (Surry Hills) was tunnelled beneath the burial ground. The end of Pitt Street was widened, so was the road fronting the cemetery which became Eddy Avenue.

The day set for the opening of Central Railway Station was Saturday, 4 August 1906. The Premier, the Hon J H Carruthers, was presented with a golden key to open the ticket

The new Central Railway Station, minus the clock in the 1920s. (Public Transport Commission)

office and the Minister for Works, Sir John See, blew the golden whistle at the close of his speech in which he couldn't resist mentioning the station was built in the wrong place.

The last train drew out from the old number 5 platform at midnight and additional lines were hastily laid by dawn on the Sunday. At 5.50 am the Western Mail chuffed through to the new station which remained a disappointment for commuters who had to find their own transport to the city centre. They were somewhat appeased in 1926, with the opening the city circle line.

A familiar view of Eddy Avenue from George Street, in front of the Great Southern Hotel, in September 1923. (NSW Government Printer)

Tollgate Gothic

The first tollgate was erected at the top of George Street, today's Railway Square, in 1811 replaced by Francis Greenway's 'barricade' in 1819. Its Gothic proportions were said to fill wayfarers with awe but critics of Governor Macquarie and his architect considered it an extravagant trifle. 'An inelegant and fugacious toy' sniffed rival architect Henry Kitchen.

The tollgate, with accommodation for the toll keeper, was leased by tender on a 12-month basis. The distance from the toll to Parramatta being measured at 14 miles. Monsieur Peron, a visiting French explorer, journeyed along the road in 1802: 'This grand road appears at a distance like an immense avenue of foliage and verdure. A charming freshness and agreeable shade always prevails in this continuous bower, the silence of which is interrupted only by the singing and chirping of the richly plumed paroquets [sic] and other birds which inhabit it.'

Just as well Monsieur Peron is not around to see Parramatta Road as it is today. The tollgate was removed a mile south alongside Grose Farm, now Sydney University grounds, in 1836 and later still further to Annandale. All tolls were abolished in 1878 but were reintroduced to pay for the Sydney Harbour Bridge in 1932.

Left: Greenway's toll bar stood at the junction of George and Pitt Streets. A police office was built on the site followed, in 1906, by Marcus Clarke's department store and later the NSW Lottery Office.

Cars and carts in Railway Square 1916.

Railway Square in 1920. Marcus Clarke's department store can be seen on the corner of Pitt and George. This was the location of the first toll gate. (NSW Government Printer)

Bibliography

A Century of Journalism 1831-1931 (John Fairfax and Sons)
APPERLY, R & LIND, P, *444 Sydney Buildings* (Angus & Robertson 1971)
ASHTON, P & WATERSON, D, *Sydney Takes Shape, a History in Maps* (Hema Maps 2000)
BARNARD, Marjorie, *Sydney: Story of a City* (Melbourne University Press 1956)
BERGMAN, G F J & LEVI, J S, *Australian Genesis* (Rigby 1974)
BIRCH & MACMILLAN, *The Sydney Scene 1788-1960* (Hale and Iremonger 1982)
BIRMINGHAM, J & LISTON, C, *Old Sydney Burial Ground 1974* (ASCHA 1976)
BIRMINGHAM, J, *Leviathan, the unauthorised biography of Sydney* (Random House, 1999)
BRAND, Simon, *Picture Palaces and Flea Pits* (Dreamweaver Books 1983)
BROADBENT, J & EVANS, I, *The Golden Decade of Australian Architecture* (David Ell, 1978)
BRODSKY, Isadore, *Streets of Sydney* (Old Sydney Free Press 1974)
BRODSKY, Isadore, *Sydney Looks Back* (Angus and Robertson 1957)
BRODSKY, Isadore, *Sydney Press Gang* (Old Sydney Free Press 1974)
BRODSKY, Isadore, *Sydney Takes the Stage* (Old Sydney Free Press 1963)
BRODSKY, Isadore, *Sydney's Phantom Book Shops* (University Co-Op Bookshop 1973)
Centenary History of the NSW Police Force (NSW Government Printer 1962)
CHRISTIE, M, *The Sydney Markets 1788-1988* (Sydney Market Authority 1988)
CLARK, C M H, *History of Australia* (Melbourne University Press 1962-1987)
CLUNE, Frank, *Saga of Sydney* (NSW Government Tourist Bureau 1961)
CLUNE, Frank, *Serenade to Sydney* (Angus and Robertson 1967)
CROWLEY, Frank, *Colonial Australia Vol 1, 2 and 3* (Thomas Nelson 1980)
CUNNINGHAM, Peter, *Two Years in NSW* (1827 facsimile Angus and Robertson 1966)
DE VRIES, S, *Historic Sydney the Founding of Australia* (Pandanus Press 1983)
DOW, Gwyneth, *Samuel Terry* (Sydney University Press 1974)
ELLIS, M A, *Francis Greenway* (Angus and Robertson 1949)
ELLIS, M A, *Lachlan Macquarie* (Angus and Robertson 1947)
EVANS, Susanna, *Historical Sydney as Seen by Early Artists* (Doubleday 1983)
EVATT, H V, *Rum Rebellion* (Lloyd O'Neill 1971)
FITZGERALD, *Red Tape, Gold Scissors* (SLNSW Press 1997)
FORBES, George, *History of Sydney* (William Brooks 1926)
FORD, J, *Meet Me at the Trocadero* (J Ford, 1995)
FORSYTH, John, *How and Why of Station Names* (State Rail Authority 1986)
FOWLES, Joseph, *Sydney in 1848* (1848 facsimile Ure Smith 1962)
FREELAND, J M, *Architecture in Australia* (Cheshire 1968)
FREELAND, J M, *The Australian Pub* (Melbourne University Press 1966)
GILBERT, Lionel, *The Royal Botanic Gardens Sydney 1816-1985* (Oxford University Press 1986)
Gregory's Street Directory (1986)
GROOM, B & WICKHAM, W, *The Lost Collections* (University of Sydney 1982)

HEATON, J H, *Australian Dictionary of Dates* (George Robertson 1879)
The Heritage of Australia (Macmillan 1981)
HERMAN, Morton, *The Blackets* (Angus and Robertson 1963)
HERMAN, Morton, *Early Australian Architects and their Work* (Angus and Robertson 1954)
Historical Records of Australia (Library Committee of the Commonwealth Parliament 1914)
HUGHES, J, *Demolished Houses of Sydney* (Historic Houses Trust of NSW 1999)
HUGHES, Robert, *The Fatal Shore* (Collins Harvill 1987)
IRVIN, Eric, *Dictionary of Australian Theatre 1788-1914* (Hale and Iremonger 1985)
JOHNSTONE, S M, *Book of St Andrew's Cathedral* (Angus and Robertson 1937)
KERR, J S, *Design for Convicts* (Library of Australian History 1984)
KERR, Joan, *Edmund Thomas Blacket* (National Trust of Australia 1983)
KENNEDY, Brian & Barbara, *Subterranean Sydney* (A H and A W Reed 1982)
LATTA, D, *Lost Glories, a memorial to forgotten Australian buildings* (Angus & Robertson 1986)
MACQUARIE, Lachlan, *Journal of His Tours in NSW 1810-1822* (LAH, 1979)
The Mitchell Library (Trustees of the Public Library of NSW 1936)
O'FARRELL, P (ed), *St Mary's Cathedral Sydney 1821-1971* (Devonshire Press 1971)
PARK, Ruth, *Companion Guide to Sydney* (Collins 1973)
Phillip Geeves presents Cazneaux's Sydney 1904-1934 (David Ell 1980)
RICHARDS, Thomas, *NSW 1881* (Government Printer 1881)
ROE, Jill, *Twentieth Century Sydney* (Hale and Iremonger 1980)
Sand's Directory (1867, 1888, 1924)
SCOTT, Geoffrey, *Sydney's Highways of History* (Georgian House 1958)
SELKIRK PROVIS, J & JOHNSON, K A, *Cadman's Cottage* (privately published 1972)
SHAW, Harvey, *From the Quay* (NSW University Press 1981)
SHAW, John, *The Queen Victoria Building* (Wellington Lane Press 1987)
SMITH, V, *The Sydney Opera House* (Summit Books 1977)
SPEARRITT, Peter, *Sydney Since the Twenties* (Hale and Iremonger 1978)
STANBURY, Peter (ed), *10 000 Years of Sydney Life* (Macleay Museum 1979)
SUTTON, Ralph, *Soldiers of the Queen* (NSW Military Historical Society 1985)
THORNE, Russ, *Picture Palace Architecture* (Sun Books 1976)
THORNE, Russ, *Theatre Buildings of Australian Architecture* (University of Sydney 1971)
TURNER, J, *Joseph Lycett Governor Macquarie's convict artist* (Hunter History Pub. 1997)
TYRRELL, James, *Old Books, Old Friends, Old Sydney* (Angus and Robertson 1952)
View and Description of the Town of Sydney 1827 (Library of Australian History 1978)
WALKER, R B, *The Newspaper Press in NSW 1803-1920* (Sydney University Press 1976)
WATSON, J F, *The History of Sydney Hospital 1811-1911* (Government Printer 1911)
Wilson's Street Directory (1918)

Index

Abrahams. Esther 37
Adam's Hotel 83
Adelaide Steamship Co. 70
Albert Street 7
Allwood, Robert 56
Anderson, Robert 44
Angus and Robertson 51, 100, 101
Angus, David 100
Annandale 37
Anthony Hordern stores 73, 106, 122, 123
Appleton, Charles 70
Archibald, J.F. 62, 63
Argyle Cut 17, 20, 21
Australia Hotel 71, 98, 104, 105, 106. 107
Australian 57
Australian Museum 67
Australian Star 106
Australian Subscription Library 77
Australasian Union Steamship Co 6
Ballantyre, Cedric 120
Balmain 39
Bank of NSW 10
Banks, Joseph 44
Barnard, Marjorie 63
Barnet, James 13, 47 97
Barney, George 8
Barrack Street 29, 112
Bathurst 10
Bathurst, Lord 41
Bavin, T.R. 90
Bean, C.W.E.101
Beard Watson 112
Belmore Family Hotel 9
Belmore Markets 125
Bennelong Point 25
Bennett, George 66
Bent Street 33
Berkelouw's Bookshop 108
Bernhardt, Sarah 103, 106
Bibb, John 72

Bidwell, John 44
Bigge, Commissioner 3, 39 41, 55, 56, 58 119
Blacket, Edmund 13, 31,119
Blaxcell, Garnham 52
Bligh, Governor William 3, 5, 6, 10, 36, 37, 40, 43
Blore, Edward 42, 43
Bluett, Gus 105
Bonwick, James 30
Botanic Gardens, 22, 43, 44, 47
Botany Cemetery 30
Bounty 37
Bourke, Richard 28, 40, 119
Bowman, James 53
Bradfield, J.J.C. 23
Bridge Street 4, 8, 36, 37, 38, 39, 69
Brown, Thomas 102
Builders' Labourers' Federation 90
Bulletin 62, 63
Cadman's Cottage 7
Cadrigal tribe 1
Cahill, Joseph 26
Cahill Expressway 11, 15, 116
Campbell, Robert 6, 30
Campbell Street 17, 126, 127
Campbell's Wharf 6, 20
Campbelltown 58
Capitol Theatre 120, 124, 125
Carruthers, Joseph 50, 133
Castlereagh Street 8, 31, 101,104, 105
Centennial Park 4, 22
Central Railway Station 14, 30
Christmas, Percy 80
Circular Quay 3, 4, 5, 7, 8, 9, 10, 14, 15, 20, 24, 42
Clarence Street 29, 30
Clarke, William Branwhite 47, 66
Clegg, Harry 129
Cockatoo Island 55
College Street 58, 72
Collins, David 37
Commissariat Stores 5

Conrad, Joseph 38
Conservatorium of Music 41, 47, 48
Cook, James 1
Coughlan, Frank 121
Cowper, William 31
Crimean War 25
Crossley, George 94
Cumberland Street 20
Cummings, William 33
Cunningham, Richard 43, 44
Cureton, Edward 39
Customs House 10, 11
Dally-Watkins, June 99
Darling, Ralph 7, 10, 31, 56, 57, 58, 68, 128
Darling Harbour 20, 102, 125, 127, 128, 129
Darlinghurst Courthouse 57
Darlinghurst Gaol 62
Darlinghurst Road 50
Darwin, Charles 66
David Jones 56, 58, 70, 112
Davidson, E.J. 56
Dawes Point 20, 25, 52
De Chair, Dudley 90
De Groot, Francis van 23
De Luca, Guiseppe 108
Denison, Sir William 38, 132
Dennis, C.J. 63, 100
Devonshire Street Cemetery 7, 30
Domain 43, 50
Dorman Long & Co Ltd 23
Doyle, Stuart 90, 120, 124
Duke of Edinburgh 53, 102, 118, 119
Dundas, Jane 30
Duntroon 6
Dymock's Book Arcade 99, 108
East India Company 6
Eastern Suburbs Railway 94
Eddy Avenue 133
Elizabeth Street 8, 58, 61
Embassy Cinema 104, 105
Essex Street 18, 28, 30

Fairfax, John 76, 77
Farm Cove 43
Farmer and Company 83, 86
Fink, Leo 120
Foley, Larry 81
Follar, Charles 102
Forbes, Sir Francis 57
Ford, Joan 121
Forsyth, Marjory 99
Fort Macquarie 25
Frankenstein, Rosa 62
Fraser, Charles 44
Gaby, James 131
Galvin, William 66
Garden Island 5
Garden Palace 47, 48, 49
Garrick Theatre 104
Geeves, Philip 98
General Post Office 94, 96, 97
George Street 7, 8, 17, 20, 28, 29, 30, 32, 37, 40, 69, 83, 116, 117, 119, 120, 122, 123
George Street Barracks 30
George Street Markets 114, 115
George the Third 31, 36
Gibbs, John 10
Gibbs, Shallard & Co 94
Gibson, William 73
Gilmore, Mary 63
Gipps, George 10, 42, 44, 66, 118
Gloucester Street 18
Goossens, Eugene 26
Government House 3, 8, 20, 42
Greater Union Theatres 90, 120, 124
Great Synagogue 69, 98
Green Ban 22
Greenway, Francis 3, 7, 39, 41, 52, 55, 56, 57, 116, 119
Gresham Hotel 114
Grose Farm 135
Grosvenor Street 30
Halfpenny Bridge 8
Hall, Edward Smith 56
Halstead Press 101

Hamilton, Gavin 30
Harbour Bridge 19, 20, 23, 24
Harris, John 116, 118
Haskell, Arnold 106
Haymarket 123,127
Haynes, John 62
Her Majesty's Arcade 81
Her Majesty's Theatre 106,124
Hilton Hotel 81, 83, 117
Hippodrome 124
Historic Houses Trust 42, 55
History House 47
Holiday Inn 32
Holmes, William 66
Hopkins, Livingstone 62
Horne, Donald 63
Hosking, John 94, 118
Howe, George 40
Hughes, George 40
Hughes, Billy 94, 133
Hunter, John 4, 28, 31, 52, 96
Hunter Street 4, 30, 31, 74, 75
Hyde Park, 4, 43, 59, 60, 64, 65, 72
Hyde Park Barracks 20, 53, 55, 56, 119
Illustrated Sydney News 93, 94
Imperial Arcade 80, 81, 86
Jevons, William 17
Johnson, Richard 31
Johnston, George 6, 37
Jones, Richard 40 74
Kelly, Ned 108
Kelly, Theo 80
Kemp, Charles 76, 77
Kent Street 20, 29
King, Billy 108
King, Philip Gidley 4, 40, 108
King Street 4, 58, 108, 109, 110, 111
Kitchen, Henry 135
Krefft, Johann Ludwig Gerrard 66
Lachlan Swamps 4
Lane, Tim 20
Lang, Jack 23
Lang, John Dunmore 33

Lavender Bay 28
Lawson, Henry 62, 100
Lewis, Mortimer 66
Levey, Barnett 69, 99
Lewis, Mortimer 10, 42
Lewis, Thomas 106, 108
Lindsay, Norman 62, 101
Liverpool Street 72
Lloyd, Marie 105
Loftus, Lord 47, 53
Lord, Simeon 4, 39
Low, David 62
Lycett, Joseph 2
Lyons Terrace 72
Macarthur, John 6, 10, 37, 52
McCrae, Hugh 63
McDowell's Store 112
McLeod, William 62
Mackellar, Dorothea 63
Macleay, Alexander 66, 68
Maclehose, James 74, 116
Macquarie, Lachlan 3, 5, 6, 25, 29, 36, 37, 39, 40, 41, 43, 44, 52, 55, 56, 57, 58, 65, 96, 116, 119, 128
Macquarie Lighthouse 55
Macquarie Place 4, 36, 39, 40
Macquarie Street 36, 41 - 57
Maiden, Joseph Henry 44
Manning, Emily 50
Marcus Clarke 73, 135, 136
Margaret Street 29, 30, 32
Mariner's Church 15
Maritime Museum 12, 128
Market Street 4, 30, 58, 83
Mark Foy 73
Martin Place Plaza 91, 92, 93, 94, 95, 96, 97
Martin, James 94
May, Phil 62
Menzies Hotel 32
Metropolitan Hotel 94
Mitchell, David Scott 50, 51, 99
Mitchell Library 47, 50, 51, 99
Mitchell, Thomas 43, 68
MLC Centre 103

Moncrieff, Gladys 105
Montez, Lola 102
Moore, Carrie 105
Moore, Charles 44
Moore, Edwin 104, 106
Moore Park 22
Mort, Thomas Sutcliffe 9, 39
Mundey, Jack 22
Museum of Sydney 36
National Parks and Wildlife Service 7
National Trust 4, 90
NSW Builders Federation 22
NSW Corps 6
NSW Heritage Council 120, 124
Nichols, Isaac 96
Nicholsons Music Store 112
Norfolk Island 10, 39, 96
Norton, John 106
O'Connell, Maurice 29
O'Sullivan, Edward 133
Opera House 25, 26, 27, 97
Orient Hotel 5
Oxford Hotel 106, 108
Packer, Frank 63, 106
Paddington 30
Paddy's Market 127
Palings Music Store 112
Palmer, John 5
Palmer, Vance 63
Parkes, Sir Henry 47, 53, 97, 99, 104, 106
Paris Cinema 72
Paterson, Banjo 62, 100
Petty's Hotel 31, 33, 104
Phillip, Arthur 3, 4, 5, 25, 30, 31, 36, 40, 43
Phillip Street 7, 8, 9, 13, 36
Phoenix 28
Piccadilly Arcade 81
Piper, John 10
Pitt Street 4, 8, 30, 38, 78, 79, 82, 83, 84, 85, 86, 87, 88, 89
Playbox Theatre 98
Playfair Building 22

Point Piper 10
Pritchard, Katherine Susannah 63
Prince Edward Theatre 71
Prince of Wales Theatre 102
Princes Restaurant 94
Princes Street 19, 20, 22
Prior, Samuel 63
Pulteney Hotel 33, 104, 118
Putland, Mary 36
Pyrmont Bridge 128, 130
Queen Victoria 25
Queen Victoria Building 80, 114, 115, 116, 117
Quong Tart's Tea rooms 103, 108
Rae, John 41
Railway Square 135, 136
Raymond, James 97
Redfern, William 29, 40, 53
Regent Theatre 120
Rene, Roy 105
Rickards, Harry 104
Reiby, Mary 106
Richardson and Wrench 38
Riley, Alexander 52
Roach, John 66
Robertson, George 99, 100
Rocks 17, 19, 20, 22, 28
Rose, Thomas 58
Rowe Street 98
Royal Arcade 81, 83
Royal Exchange 38
Royal George Hotel 130
Royal Hotel 99, 104
Royal Park Hotel
Royal Prince Alfred Hospital 53
Royal Victoria Theatre 102
Rum Rebellion 6
Rydge, Norman 90
St Andrews Cathedral 54, 56, 119
St Marys 54, 65
St James Church 56
St James Railway Station 56
St Phillip's Church 31
Sargent's 112
Scandinavian Theatre 104

Scot's Church 31, 33
See, John 133
Sirius 5, 39
Smith's Weekly 63
State Library of NSW 48
State Theatre 90, 104, 124
Stevens, A.G. 62
Stevens, Bertram
Stevenson, Robert Louis 33, 38
Stokes, Frederick 76, 77
Strand Arcade 81, 83
Success 12
Sussex Street 130
Sydney Arcade 81
Sydney Book Club 100
Sydney Cove Redevelopment Scheme 7, 19
Sydney Gazette 4, 40, 52, 76
Sydney Girls' High School 58
Sydney Grammar School 58
Sydney Harbour Tunnel 23
Sydney Hospital 98
Sydney Monitor 56
Sydney Morning Herald 40, 47, 76
Tank Stream 3, 4, 8, 37
Taronga Park Zoo 44
Tawell, John 74
Terry, Samuel 94, 97
Theatre Royal 99, 103
Thring, Frank 120
Tivoli Theatre 104, 105
Town Hall 30, 118
Trocadero 121
Traill, W.H. 62
Truth 108
Tyrrell, James 50, 100
Utzon, Joern 26
Verge, John 56, 72
Vernon, W.L. 41
Victoria Hall 104
Wentworth Avenue 72
Wentworth, D'Arcy 52, 53
White, Henry 124
White Horse Tavern 81
Whitlam, Gough 94

William Street 68
Williamson, J C 103, 105, 120
Woolloomooloo 5, 22
Woolworths 80
Wyatt, Colin 66
Wyatt, Joseph 102
Wymark, Frederick 51
Wynyard Station 29
Wynyard Square 29, 33, 34, 35, 97
York Street 29, 33, 114
Young, John 102

Available at all good bookstores and newsagents. If unavailable please phone (02) 9557 4367

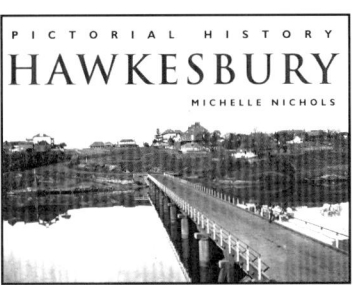

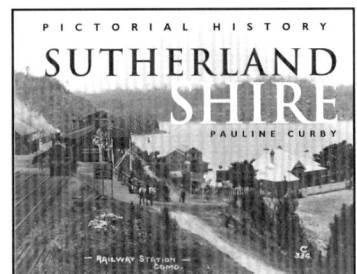

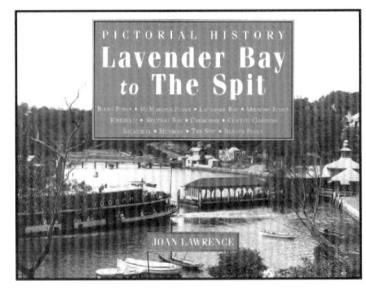

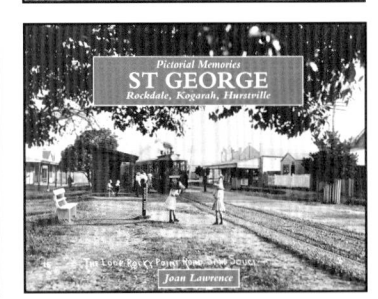

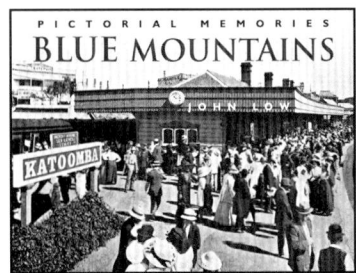

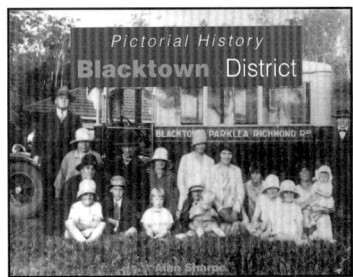

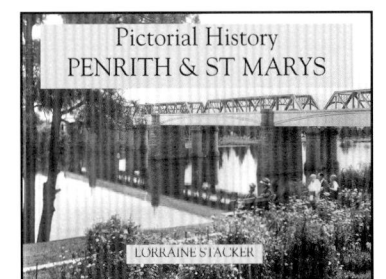

Forthcoming titles: Cronulla, Lower North Shore, Wollongong and Marrickville
Kingsclear Books PO Box 335, Alexandria 1435.
Email kingsclear@wr.com.au / www.kingsclearbooks.com.au.